CONCILIUM

RELIGION AND IDENTITY IN POST-CONFLICT SOCIETIES

Edited by

Regina Ammicht Quinn, Mile Babić,

Zoran Grozdanov, Susan A. Ross

& Marie-Therese Wacker

SCM Press · London

Published in 2015 by SCM Press, 3rd Floor, Invicta House,
108–114 Golden Lane, London EC1Y 0TG.

SCM Press is an imprint of Hymns Ancient & Modern Ltd (a registered charity)
13A Hellesdon Park Road, Norwich NR6 5DR, UK

ISBN 9780334031321

Printed in the UK by
Ashford Press, Hampshire

Contents

Editorial
Religion and Identity in
Post-conflict Societies

The question of religion and identity dates back almost to the beginning of humankind. Throughout history, religion has often been linked to identity, with religion playing the role of support or advocate of the dominant politics.

We needn't go far to find many examples of pernicious relationships between religion and political as well as social identity. The most recent historically in the European context is that of the ex-Yugoslavian conflict, where the wars were not religious (although some historians and scientists claim otherwise), but were fought with the aims of territorial conquest and establishing an ethnically-clean territory. Yet religion often served to initiate the conflicts, and soldiers went to war with their weapons blessed, and prayed not for the end of the war but for victory over the enemy.

Moreover, in very complex identity constructions, especially in those areas where national, ethnical and political identities are closely related historically and politically, to each other and to the religious identities of individuals and communities, it is sometimes very hard to draw a clear line between religious and all other identities that define the members of a particular society. Then we have to ask how religion can become and remain the main moving force of non-violent action, reconciliation and the search for justice in societies affected by war or major conflicts, and how religion can act as the healing factor in those societies. These goals and motives are bound to collide with national and/or ethnic aims in societies where ethnic and national identities are closely interwoven with religious identities. The associated doubts and concerns and the need to find a key to these relationships constitute a major challenge to religious institutions and individuals in societies which take part in direct conflict, whether recently in ex-Yugoslavia, or elsewhere, in the Philippines or South Africa for instance.

This situation largely accounted for the decision of the *International*

7

Journal of Theology Concilium to hold its 2014 annual meeting in Sarajevo, the symbol and scene of the greatest conflict in Europe after World War II, and the place where the First World War, the 'Great War' of 1914–18, was initiated. *Concilium*, the International Centre for Ethics in the Sciences of Tübingen, Germany (IZEW) and the Franciscan Faculty of Theology, Sarajevo, also organized a conference there on 'Theology in a Post-conflict Society: Religion and Identity' on the occasion of the hundredth anniversary of the beginning of the First World War, and under the auspices of the City of Sarajevo.

The problem of identity, especially with regard to the host country, Bosnia and Herzegovina, consists of a multitude of entwined religious, ethnic and political components. Therefore authors and experts from various backgrounds, with respect to their world-views as well as their specialisms, were invited to address the Conference. Problems of religion and identity were dealt with by the novelists Aleksandar Hemon and Dževad Karahasan; Catholic theologians Felix Wilfred, Mile Babić, Regina Ammicht Quinn, Daniel Pilario, Pero Sudar and Erik Borgman; Orthodox theologian Pantelis Kalaitzidis; Protestant theologians Miroslav Volf and Sarojini Nadar; the Islamic representative Dževad Hodžić, the philosopher Ugo Vlaisavljević, and the sociologist Dino Abazović. The aim was to examine from various perspectives questions of identity construction, the definition of the boundaries and expression of identity, and the influence of religious attitudes and beliefs on individual and collective identity in a particular social and political framework. The participants covered not only the recent war in ex-Yugoslavia (1991–5) but conflicts around the world, and the fundamental relations between individual and/ or community identities and religion in European and global contexts. We are grateful to all the participants for agreeing to rework their papers for this issue of *Concilium*.

The Theological Forum in this *Concilium* includes three articles. Klaus Raupp writes about a book, Thomas Piketty's *Capital for the Twenty-first Century*, which has aroused considerable interest and controversy in the field of economy. Stipe Odak looks at a recent book by a group of young Croatian and Bosnian theologians on the fortieth anniversary of the publication of *The Crucified God*, Jürgen Moltmann's theological classic. The Forum closes with a reflection by two Croatian theologians, Jadranka Rebeka Anić and Jadranka Brnčić, on a document *On Gender Ideology* issued by the Croatian Bishops' Conference.

Editorial

We wish to thank the conference organizers and Norbert Reck and Luis Carlos Susin for their help in preparing this issue.

Regina Ammicht Quinn, Mile Babić, Zoran Grozdanov,
Susan A. Ross, Marie-Therese Wacker

Part One: The Puzzle of Identity

Dilemmas and Trajectories of Peace

FELIX WILFRED

So-called religious conflicts are complex and have to be situated in their social, political and cultural contexts, where identities compete on the basis of ethnicity, language, religion, history, sub-nationalities and so on. Religion is an important marker of identity. It also supplies symbols, myths and emotional power for conflicts instrumentalized by vested interests. It is caught in a dilemma between conflict and a vocation for peace. To become genuine builders of peace, religions must take into account the fluid and porous nature of all identities, including the religious variety; cultivate a sense of multi-layered identity in the life of individuals and communities; join forces with civil-society initiatives and social movements; promote equity and justice; and help to heal memories and rewrite history. All this calls for a new educational praxis by religions.

I Introduction

Conflicts based on ethnic and religious identities have continued to cause the loss of a vast number of precious human lives, many of them buried in mass-graves. They have resulted in many injured and maimed people, forced expulsions, genocide and ethnic cleansing, refugees, and missing and displaced people; mass rape and sexual assault; and destruction of places of worship and cultural symbols. These conflicts have been real tragedies with crimes against humanity, as shown by wars in Bosnia and Herzegovina, Kosovo, Sri Lanka and many African nations.

The challenge for all religions today is to refrain from violence, draw from their own resources and contribute to the cause of peace. There is no need to fear religion as long as it can build peace. But this cannot be done simply by preaching. Religion is not an isolated entity, for it is immersed in other political, economic and cultural social systems and forces.

II Religion and ethnic identity

Religion, at least theoretically, may not figure anywhere in a modern Western society claiming to live by Enlightenment ideals and promoting individual freedom and the construction of an autonomous self ('individualization'). At the most, religion would belong to the realm of one's free choice rather than that of something inherited and inherent in one's self and collective identity, culture and tradition. For most people, religion is a very important marker of their identity, as it often represents some of the ultimate values and ideals they hold on to.

There are many societies in which religion overlaps with ethnic identity. Serb and Orthodox identities overlap, like Croatian and Catholic, Bosnian and Islamic identities. In Sri Lanka, the ethnic identity of the Sinhalese is a Buddhist religious identity, whereas Tamil identity is Hindu. In Malaysia, to be Malay is to be a Muslim; to be Indian is to be a Hindu; and to be Chinese is to be a Confucian. With multiple religious and ethnic identities, we have to ask in which image the modern nation-State is to be fashioned, and ultimately this is a question of power. Even at the heart of Europe, there is an undercurrent of right-wing opinion that to be European is to be Christian (*pace* secularists!) and for some people 'European Muslim' is a strange and intolerable proposal. It would appear that this kind of thinking was bolstered for some time at least during the Bosnian war.

Although people in everyday life interact across religious borders, there are times when ethnic identities very often come into conflict for political, economic, and cultural reasons. At this juncture, the religious factor adds strong emotional intensity to the conflict, provides symbols and narratives, and exacerbates the relationship between ethnic communities in the same nation. The political ambitions of elites, for example, are an important factor in religio-ethnic conflicts. The instrumentalization of religious extremism helps them to trump up mass support.

When religious identity becomes the singular, overwhelming and comprehensive identity, it is prone to cause conflicts and violence. We also should admit that in the same societies where religion plays the role of identity-marker, we have individuals who distance themselves from the negative aspects of religion and exercise respect, understanding, and compassion towards the religious other, reaching to the humanity in every person rather than getting bogged down in socially constructed identities. These individuals play a critical role vis-à-vis their own communities.

III Configuration of identities

Identity, broadly speaking, is the crystallization of the unique elements and characteristics that distinguish one person from another. Since human beings are both individuals and collectivities, there is, obviously, a self-identity as well as a group 'we'-identity. It is important to note that a person has multiple identities or layers of identities. When people assert a single identity, for various reasons (threat, perception of injustice, or past memories), conflicts arise, become more intense and can end in protracted violence. The shaping of identity is both internal and external. Through the socialization process, people construct their self-identities as belonging to a group and sharing some important common features with it. The construction of the other's identity often uses clichés and stereotypes, which form part of the socialization process and are deeply embedded in the psyche of the individual and of the collectivity.

With regard to identity, we should also pay attention to internal differentiation within the same religion. These differences are often so marked that two streams or denominations may be in conflict and cause violence in the same religion. For example, Protestantism and Catholicism may be locked in conflict as shown not only by history but by more recent experiences in Ireland. The Sunni and Shiite branches within the same religion of Islam may be identity markers for two different groups and one may clash violently with the other.

IV Perspectives of East and West

With regard to identity, in the West itself there is a difference between Eastern Europe and parts of Western Europe. There are similar features, for example, in Bosnia and Herzegovina, a country of many faiths, and the Asian situation. The relationship between different identities – ethnic, cultural, and religious – is very much shaped by the particular history and context. As long as there was an empire administered centrally, local identities did not play any significant role. Each identity tried to understand itself in relation to the major unit of the empire.

In Europe, there was a great multiplicity of national and ethnic identities under the Austro-Hungarian Empire. Under the Ottoman Empire the *dhimmi* system served as a safeguard against inter-ethnic and religious conflicts. In India, there was the Mughal Empire followed by the British Empire. During the imperial period, for the reason I have cited,

15

there were practically no significant religious or ethnic conflicts. Once the empire collapsed, and there was local autonomy, then competition began among the various identities in a struggle for power and to garner the best resources available. The leftist claim that ethnic and religious identity would vanish with the affirmation of a class-approach and uprisings by workers and peasants has been found to be false.

V   Fluid and porous vs stagnating identities

Identities are not to be viewed as ready-made boxes. Rigid, neatly defined and well-marked identities inevitably lead to their defence. The historical reality is that identities have not been fixed but porous. There have been different types of interaction and levels of interchange among peoples of different religious affiliations. These cannot all be set aside. Empirical studies show how, for example, there has been much interchange and communication even in the realm of worship and symbolism, as illustrated by popular religiosity. People across religious borders appropriate their neighbours' ideals, values, and symbols. In short, a dynamic and flexible understanding of identity can help prevent religious conflicts.

Stagnating identities are dangerous as they can be the breeding-ground for violence. Ossified identity seeks to secure a space for itself out of fear of the other, and would even go as far as ethnic cleansing to make sure of an exclusive space. If religions foment this kind of identity, the results can be disastrous.

VI   Promoting multiple identities

Once we are freed from stagnating identities, we see that people have multiple identities in real life. Ethnic, religious and linguistic identities are aspects of the many layers of identity with which people live their everyday lives. Their multiple identities shift, and often intersect and criss-cross, leaving little room for an insulated identity. Religions tend to be all-encompassing, and therefore to see religious identity as the singular and overarching form of identity. Hence for the most part religions have fostered exclusive identities. The new role religions need to play is to help people free themselves from a singular religious identity and forge relationships with their neighbours, not simply as religious believers but as concerned human beings and citizens sharing the same context, history

16

and conditions of everyday life. Instead of trapping people in a monolithic religious identity, an effort must be made to help them feel at home and interact with a plurality of shifting and intersecting identities.

VII   Civil society initiatives

We need a development of civil-society initiatives, in which various identities and groups participate and share many things in common. It has been observed that some cities in India are prone to Hindu–Muslim riots, whereas others are more peaceful, in spite of provocation. Why this difference? There can be many explanatory factors. However, wherever there have been different forms of inter-communitarian associational life and civil-society initiatives, voluntary agencies, and inter-ethnic marriages, there have been fewer conflicts and fewer spates of violence. These everyday practices nurture inter-ethnic and inter-religious understanding and mutuality, help build durable structures of peace, and above all, create trust among competing identities. I believe that more intense interactions in civil society could help restrain the forces of conflict and violence.

I come from a country which has been characterized by outbursts of violence, and riots among Hindus and Muslims, on the basis of culture, ethnicity, and religion. I am able to understand how disastrous conflicts could burst out in the Bosnian-Herzegovinian situation. To sustain peace, harmony and concord among competing identities in a post-conflict situation, with lingering trauma, is challenging. There is always the looming danger of repeating the past at micro- and macro-levels. Peace is a very fragile reality, and it requires perpetual vigilance. There is a need for re-education of all the identities involved. It is necessary to take a varied approach to sustaining peace. As I noted earlier, religions could come out more strongly and critically in the service of peace. This is done not only by drawing resources from religious traditions, but by helping to activate civil-society initiatives across identities and by cultivating a sense of common good.

VIII   Economic justice and equal opportunities

In situations where religious identities are locked in conflict, to escape from the tangle the situation must be healed by addressing the issue of economic justice and equal opportunities. In many societies, competition for scarce resources sets different groups against one another and identity becomes a weapon in the service of claims.

One important aspect of conflict is that it often derives from unequal economic developments among particular groups and ethnicities, causing a strongly-felt perception of injustice and deprivation. As many analyses show, if the economy weakens, submerged ethnic passions begin to emerge and tensions flare up. Things get worse when the identities receive unequal shares of economic benefits. Development needs to take place for all, independent of ethnic or religious identity. Moreover, the structural causes of inequality also have to be analyzed and addressed. In short, the conditions for long-lasting peace among multi-ethnic, multi-religious and multi-linguistic groups are provided when appropriate ways and means for equitable development are put in place. A lack of employment and of opportunities, low wages and corruption are common issues which must be addressed across ethnic and religious divides.

IX   Recognizing difference

Identity has become a major global issue that is politically loaded and has ramifications in all areas of life. There is a temptation to find easy solutions by steamrolling the different identities in favour of a misconceived model of unity and peace. Practising the exhortation to 'love one's neighbour as oneself' might have been relatively easy when the neighbour was someone belonging to one's own tribe or ethnic, religious, national, cultural or linguistic group. Today we are in a situation in which our neighbour is someone with a different mode of thinking, religious belief, way of life, history and other aspirations for the future. The acid test of our conviction regarding human dignity and rights is shown in practice in multi-ethnic and multi-religious societies by our respect for the difference represented by our neighbours.

Recognizing difference should be an important component of overall educational practice. That is, it should be a major component of formal, non-formal and informal modes of education. Religions could help societies in conflict by contributing to a new educational practice of recognition of difference and respect for it. This is something more basic and fundamental than inter-religious understanding. What is at stake is not simply the sacredness of religions and their beliefs but respect for others in their difference. This is not only a matter of religion, but pertains to many other areas of life. But religion could be a catalyst for promoting education for the recognition of difference.

X   Healing memories and rewriting history

In a post-conflict situation like that of Bosnia and Herzegovina, should we think of the past, or bury it in order to move ahead? Forgetting the past is a pragmatic approach that can be attractive. On the other hand, unredeemed memory has been at work before conflicts arise, and therefore needs to be addressed. Traumatic memories and feelings continue to haunt a post-conflict situation, and act like festering wounds to vitiate life in common in society. Truth and history must be confronted if effective healing is to occur.

The healing of memories could be a positive role for religions in conflict and post-conflict situations. Religions could help to remove the sting of revenge and hatred, and thus contribute to social harmony and cohesion. Of course, justice needs to be done, and truth should come out in the open as a prerequisite for peace and harmony in any wounded society like that of Bosnia and Herzegovina. However, no amount of restorative justice can re-establish the situation before violence and destruction were unleashed. That is gone once and for all. There will always be a deficit which can be addressed only through a process of reconciliation, which remains, in Christian terms, a matter of grace.

We can see the great scope available to religions in the field of reconciliation in conflict and post-conflict situations. Conflicts and violence among identities often stem from fear, insecurity and a sense of threat. Hence, the creation of trust in others is something that religion and religious agents could foster for the construction of peace.

History narrated and written through the lens of ethnic and religious identity invariably turns out to be partisan, especially in conflict and post-conflict situations. That kind of history clouds the facts and strays from the truth.

Strange to say, the current interests, concerns and aspirations of various identities condition the narrative of the past. The suffering and injustice that one group has undergone are highlighted while the suffering of another group is conveniently forgotten or made light of. History must also be redeemed by a process of rewriting in the light of truth and reconciliation in the post-conflict situation. This is indeed a very challenging task.

XI Conclusion

Some years ago, when visiting the former Dachau concentration camp, one thing in particular struck me. There I saw the statue of an emaciated prisoner which probably represented the thousands of innocent people who underwent senseless suffering and death at that spot. The inscription read: 'Den Toten zur Ehre – den Lebenden zur Mahnung': Honour to the dead, and a warning to the living. We want to remember all the people who died in the ethnic and religious war in Bosnia and Herzegovina, and in similar wars in other parts of the world. Unfortunately, religion has been an accomplice in ethnic and religious wars, if not always by sins of commission, then certainly by those of omission: its failures to do enough to prevent conflicts and to contribute to the process of peace and harmony. Religions have failed to emerge from their ambiguities. The war in Bosnia is full of lessons for all humanity, especially about what should never be repeated. There should never be another Srebrenica. It is a perpetual reminder and warning to religions and theologies that they cannot remain idle when the house is burning, but must commit themselves urgently to quenching the fire, and help to build bridges of peace and harmony in cooperation with all those of good will.

Religions, Identities and Conflicts

MIROSLAV VOLF

The principal reason why universalistic religions often end up legitimizing and motivating violence lies neither in the distinction which all universalistic religions make between true and false religion, nor in the alleged irrationality of religions, but in the entanglement of religions with political power.

I Introduction

The main sources of conflict between people are well-known. Almost four centuries ago, Thomas Hobbes might have said the last word on the matter. In the same chapter of *Leviathan* (1651) in which he famously described human life in the 'state of nature' as 'solitary, poor, nasty, brutish, and short', he identified three principal sources of conflict: competition, diffidence and glory. 'The first maketh men invade for Gain; the second, for Safety; and the third, for Reputation. The first use Violence, to make themselves Masters of other mens persons, wives, children, and cattell; the second, to defend them; the third, for trifles, as a word, a smile, a different opinion, and any other signe of undervalue, either direct in their Persons, or by reflexion in their Kindred, their Friends, their Nation, their Profession, or their Name.'[1]

This succinct summary of the causes of violence appears in the chapter on the pre-state condition of humanity. But Hobbes insisted that the three 'principall causes of quarrell' are rooted not in a particular social arrangement but 'in the nature of man'.[2]

Some critics of religion think that religion is a major and independent cause of violence, a fourth source of conflict in addition to Hobbes' three. In many cases they are right. Historically, however, religions have contributed to social discord and to harmony, and they have inspired and legitimized violence and peacemaking. As lived realities, religions are neither simply violent nor simply peaceable but ambivalent. The critics of religion recognize this ambivalence but have ready explanations of it: to temper their inherent violent proclivities, religions have tended to reach for the milk of human kindness or for the Enlightenment value of tolerance.[3] Many defenders of religions recognize the ambivalence, but believe that the problem lies in a basic flaw of human nature; self-interested as we humans are, when it suits our interests – our desire for gain, security, and reputation – we twist that which is best into the worst of all; in the hands of evil men and women, what is holy becomes daemonic.[4]

II Religions and violence

Critics give two main reasons why major world religions have, as they see it, a strong proclivity to violence. First, for most world religions the distinctions between true and false religion, and between justice and injustice or good and evil, are central. They affirm the goodness of the way of life they seek to follow and therefore reject others as imperfect, misguided, or even wicked. Second, in their own self-understanding, most world religions are based either on positive revelation or on spiritual enlightenment; reason stops at some point, critics object, and gives way to mere conviction. It follows that major world religions are marked by irrational certainty. Moreover, unlike rationality, which all humans possess, revelation or enlightenment belongs only to a relatively select few. World religions divide humanity into an in-group and an out-group. Many critics hold that insisting without sufficient reason on the truth of your own view of the ultimate reality and the way of life corresponding to it is bound to breed violence.[5]

But the distinction between true and false religion, which is tied with the concern of religion with justice, is a presupposition of responsible peace and not, as such, a cause of violence. As to the alleged irrationality of religion, the critical issue isn't that in religions reason stops at some point, giving way to conviction; for reason never goes all the way, not even in philosophy or science. The critical issue is the content of religious teachings, for instance, whether they urge you to be merciful and love your enemies or kill the infidel, heretic, or transgressor.[6] But the defenders of religions aren't entirely correct either. It is too easy merely to blame corrupt human nature for religious violence. The connection between religion and violence is too tight for us not to examine the contribution of religions themselves to violence.

Both defenders and critics miss the actual way in which religions cause violence because they tend to see religions as monolithic and static wholes; defenders deem a particular religion, all religions, to be peaceable, and critics say that they are violent. Working with a more dynamic understanding of religion, David Martin has helpfully suggested that we should think of religions as 'repertoires of linked motifs internally articulated in a distinctive manner, and giving rise to characteristic extrapolations' about a way of life in the world: repertoires that are tied back to the original revelation, enlightenment or wisdom but not identical with it.[7] Depending on a setting (for instance, features of the culture, other religions present, the needs of the political powers) and guiding interests, the character of a religion changes: some motifs from its repertoire are backgrounded, others are foregrounded, and most are 'played' with various types and degrees of consonance or dissonance with the situation. But, changing as they do, depending on circumstances, religions are not infinitely malleable. Each religion's original articulation 'creates a flexible but distinctive logic and a grammar of transformations'.[8] Original articulations place normative constraints on religions as they change depending on circumstances; they are the wellsprings of religions' internal reform.

Some forms of world religion foster violence whereas others don't. The critical question is what makes the difference. As I shall argue shortly, the main culprit is the entanglement of religions with political power, either when the original articulation was made or as it was later transmitted and received. That's what defenders or critics of religions don't see when they trace religious violence back to the basic flaw of human nature, or to exclusivism and irrationality. Why do world religions so easily get entangled with political power? Their adherents twist one constitutive feature of these religions: the claim that a particular religion is the true way of life. Instead of being content to bear witness to truth and thereby honour individuals' responsibility to embrace a way of life for themselves, the adherents of world religions use instruments of state power to subdue and compel detractors. In the process, they reconfigure the religion, foregrounding its more bellicose motives.

III Religion and society

Two Western thinkers, Thomas Hobbes and Immanuel Kant, each a source
of a dominant tradition in political philosophy, noted two major functions
of religion in society. First, religions are employed as tools of government.
Hobbes noted that rulers use religion to make it easier to rule their subjects.
To that end,with the help of religious elites, they 'nourish, dresse, and
forme' native religious inclinations (which he thought stemmed from the
fear of invisible powers), crafting religious convictions to dull people's
response to suffering, legitimize oppressive rule, and justify unjust wars.[9]
Second, religions function as markers of communal identity. Kant thought
that the varieties of religions (in addition to the diversity of languages) are
the primary way in which nature separates people into groups. As markers
of identity, religions 'bring with them the propensity to mutual hatred and
pretexts for war'.[10] These two functions of religion often merge into one.
In the conflict between Christians and Muslims in Kosovo, the birth-place
of Serbian Orthodox civilization now populated primarily by Muslim
Albanians, and in conflicts between Hindus and Muslims in Ayodhya,
at the birth-place of the god-king Rama and the site of Babri Mosque,
religions functioned, arguably, primarily as such legitimacy-granting and
aggression-motivating markers of identity.[11]

Giving Hobbes' and Kant's observations about religion in society a
sociological twist (though without linking his proposal to either), David
Martin identifies special circumstances under which religions turn violent.
'These special circumstances occur when religion becomes virtually
coextensive with society and thus with the dynamics of power, violence,
control, cohesion, and marking out of boundaries.'[12] Religions are then
not merely publicly and politically engaged; they become 'political
religions'. The temptation to blend religion, the moral and cultural self-
understanding of a group, and political power is strong, as the three together
can generate high levels of solidarity. Many commentators think that the
primary function of religion is to provide 'collective representation' of
social unity.[13] Arguably, the world religions are not 'political religions';[14]
they must be turned into markers of political identity and legitimizers of a
given government's power.

When religions become markers of group identity, they tend to
exacerbate conflicts by providing groups with the aura of the sacred,
and thus energizing and legitimizing the struggles; inversely, conflicts
between groups associated predominantly with a single religion incline

those religions to change into markers of that group's identity. Similarly, entanglement with political power pushes towards the kind of configuration of a religion's motifs that will provide the political power with legitimacy. In situations of conflict, a religion thus configured ends up justifying the group's deployment of violence.[15] This dynamic can be observed in religions that were, in their original formulation, close to a people group and power (such as Judaism and Hinduism), and in religions that were not (such as Buddhism and Christianity), as well as in a religion whose original formulation contains both a period of distance from and a period of closeness to political power (Islam).

IV Religion reconfigured

Perhaps the best recent example of such reconfiguration of a religion by tight association with a social group and political rule over it is the paradox of a Sri Lankan Buddhist monk who has taken up the gun.[16] Buddhist monks are supposed to be deeply committed to non-violence; they are required not only to refrain from killing, but to keep at a distance from armies and traffic in arms. Not so in Sri Lanka in the second half of the twentieth century. According to Stanley Tambiah, many Sri Lankan monks came to believe that 'the religion of the Buddha and the language and culture of the Sinhalese cannot flourish without a sovereign territory which is the motherland of Sri Lanka'.[17] To give legs to this belief, they embraced political Buddhism. Built on 'certain canonical sutras dealing with ideal righteous rulers' and the Buddhist goal of 'muting worldly desires', political Buddhism stood out against 'divisive party politics and ... hankering after West-inspired materialist, consumerist, and capitalist self-seeking goals', and proposed in their place 'a simpler harmonious "Buddhist way of life" in a "Buddhist democracy"' (601). In the process, 'the substantively soteriological, ethical, and normative components of canonical doctrinal Buddhism qua religion were weakened, displaced, and even distorted' (600) – not just its character 'primarily as an ego-ideal and a mental discipline for personal salvation' (601), but its characteristic stance toward violence too. As the sons of Buddha took on the identity of the 'sons of soil', their religion was reconfigured and the affirmation of violence slithered itself into a religion whose central motifs establish a strong presumption of non-violence.[18]

The single most significant factor determining whether a religion will be implicated in violence or not is this: the level of its identification with a political project and of its entanglement with the agents that strive to realize it. The more identified a religion is with a political project and with the agents of its realization, the more likely it will be for even the otherwise most peaceful religion to 'take up the gun'. To put it somewhat differently: the less a religion's central motifs determine its embodiment in the world and the more it becomes 'religion without faith' driven by concerns extrinsic to those central motifs – which in a sense is to say, the more, in a sense, secular it becomes – the more likely it is that it will turn violent.

V Conclusion

To avoid inspiring and legitimizing violence, should religions be privatized and be kept out of public life, and barred from public engagement? In my view, public engagement is distinct from entanglement with political power. As the example of the great religious democratizers in Chile, Indonesia, the Philippines, or Poland attests, it is possible for religions to inspire and help guide public engagement without turning into mere markers of identity and instruments of political power. To avoid inspiring and legitimating violence, religions should nurture a healthy sense of independence from either established or aspiring political authority, and resist reconfiguring religion so as to reduce it primarily to a political and cultural resource.

In *A Public Faith*, I have distinguished between 'thick' and 'thin' versions of religions. When they are 'thick', religions map a way of life, foster a sense of connection with the ultimate reality and sketch a moral vision embedded in an account of the self, social relations and the good; part of such a religion is an extended argument about its nature as originally given and its relation to the changing world. Arguably, all world religions were originally articulated, received, and practised as just such 'thick' religions. In contrast, religions are 'thin'; they are emptied of their moral visions and reduced to 'vague religiosity that serves primarily to energize, heal, and give meaning to the business of life whose course is shaped by factors other than religion (such as national or economic interests)'.[19] For the most part, such 'thin' religion, I propose, is created when religions identify too closely with a given community and the dynamics of its power; and such 'thin' religions are most susceptible to

26

being used as mere political and cultural resources, and occasionally even as weapons in war.

Notes

1. Thomas Hobbes, *Leviathan*, ed. C. B. MacPherson, Harmondsworth & New York, 1968, p. 185.
2. *Ibid.*, p. 185.
3. See, for instance, Stephen Pinker, *The Better Angels of Our Nature: Why Violence Has Declined*, Harmondsworth & New York, 2011, p. 678.
4. *Cf.* Keith Ward, *Religion and Human Nature*, Oxford, 1998, pp. 1–9; 'Sin', in *The Concise Oxford Dictionary of World Religions*, John Bowker (ed.), Oxford & New York, 2003.
5. Mark Juergensmeyer (in *Terror in the Mind of God: The Global Rise of Religious Violence*, Berkeley, 2003) thinks that images of the 'cosmic war' against the forces of 'chaos' and 'evil' (pp. 148–66) are present in all religions and contribute to their propensity to violence.
6. See Miroslav Volf, *A Public Faith: How Followers of Christ Should Serve the Common Good*, Grand Rapids, 2011, pp. 37–45.
7. David Martin's formulation on which I build here concerns Christianity: 'My own procedure is to treat Christianity as a specific repertoire of linked motifs, internally articulated in a distinctive manner, and giving rise to characteristic extrapolations, but rendered recognizable by some sort of reference back to the New Testament and "primitive tradition"' (David Martin, *Does Christianity Cause War?*, Oxford, 1997, p. 32).
8. D. Martin, *Does Christianity Cause War?*, *op. cit.*, p. 120.
9. T. Hobbes, *Leviathan*, *op. cit.*, pp. 168, 173. On the State's tendency to take over religion, see Monica Duffy Toft, Daniel Philpott & Timothy Shaw, *God's Century: Resurgent Religion and Global Politics*, New York, 2011, pp. 48–81.
10. Immanuel Kant, *The Perpetual Peace*, p. 336. This is not all Kant has to say about religion, of course. Kant contrasts 'the single religion' and 'historically different creeds'. As there can be no different morals but only one, Kant thought, so there can be, properly speaking, no different religions but only 'one single religion holding for all human beings and in all times'. Historical creeds, which differ 'according to differences of time and place', are at best vehicles of that one religion. It is these historical creeds that separate people and contain a propensity to hatred and war. Forces of separation and motivators of conflict, they stand in contrast not only to the single religion as a source of unification, but to 'the power of money or 'the spirit of commerce' which 'cannot coexist with war' (p. 336).
11. On religion as a marker of identity in the war in former Yugoslavia, see Miroslav Volf, *Allah: A Christian Response*, San Francisco, 2011, p. 189. On religion as marker of identity in *Ayodhya*, see Ragini Sen & Wolfgang Wagner, 'History, Emotions and Hetero-Referential Representations in Inter-Group Conflict: The Example of Hindu–Muslim Relations in India', *Papers on Social Representation* 14 (2005), p. 2.
12. D. Martin, *Does Christianity Cause War?*, *op. cit.*, p. 134.
13. See Émile Durkheim, *Elementary Forms of Religious Life*, tr. Carol Cosman, Oxford, 2001. On the Durkheimian perspective on religious violence, see Philip S. Gorski, 'Religious Violence and Peace-Making: A Meso-Level Theory', *Practical Matters Journal* 2012, available at http://practicalmattersjournal.org/issue/5/centerpieces/critical-responses-to-the-essays-on-religious-violence-and-religious-peacebuild#gorski.

14. See Miroslav Volf (with Tony Blair), *Faith and Globalization*, New Haven, 2015.

15. For a survey of issues and approaches to the relation between religion, nationalism, and violence, see Gorski/Turkmen-Devisoglu, p. 19.

16. Michael K. Jerryson and Mark Juergensmeyer, *Buddhist Warfare*, Oxford, 2010.

17. Stanley J. Tambiah, 'Buddhism, Politics, and Violence in Sri Lanka', in *Fundamentalisms and the State: Remaking Polities, Economies, and Militancy*, vol. 3 of Martin E. Marty & F. Scott Appleby (eds), *The Fundamentalism Project*, Chicago, 1993, p. 616.

18. A similar dynamic was at work in Rwanda in the years before the outbreak of violence. During Hutu rule (1961–94), church leadership was closely intertwined with the Hutu ethnic and state power structures (see Timothy Longman, *Christianity and Genocide in Rwanda*, New York & Cambridge, 2011). 'The blood of tribalism ran deeper than the blood of baptism.' (Cardinal Roger Etchegarry).

19. M. Volf, *A Public Faith, op. cit.*, p. 40.

Individual and Collective Identity

MILE BABIĆ

In this article, I try to show how the advent of pluralism in all areas and at all levels of human life produced the crisis of (individual and collective) identity. Religious and ideological pluralism is the prerequisite for any effective resolution of religious identity and its affiliations with those professing other religions and world-views. Reactions to pluralism may be both positive and negative, and may evoke fear of others (especially pathological fear). To date they have proved to be predominantly negative. The individual has been replaced by the individualistic identity, and the collective by the collectivist identity. Both forms of identity are unrelenting. The collectivist variety reduces humans to the status of mere members of the collective, while the individualistic form deprives people of all their affiliations. Both these identities lead either to aggression or to self-isolation. The individualistic identity makes an idol of the human ego, and the collectivist identity does the same for the collective. It is possible to avoid the paradigm of fear and the enforced identity only if we realize that our relation to others is essential for our identity; that 'I' depends entirely on 'you'; and that 'you' is older and more fundamental than 'I'.

I   The importance of identity

Why is identity so important as to call for an entire conference on the subject? It became an essential topic of contemporary relevance with the rise of pluralism in all areas of human life. Present-day Europe features ethnic, linguistic, cultural, political, indeed every form of pluralism, and therefore religious pluralism too. Of course, we are particularly interested in religious and ideological pluralism and accordingly in religious identity and the relation of the Christian religion to other religions and world-views. Religious and ideological pluralism is something we constantly

29

experience, as the theologians Christoph Schwöbel[1] and Thomas Bremer[2] emphasize. Pluralism is an empirical fact, we might say. But it is both an ontological and a religious fact, so that pluralism may be grounded and justified philosophically and theologically. If you profess an authentic pluralism, you refuse all claims to a privileged centre, irrespective of the source of those claims. Authentic pluralism threatens no one's identity. If you deny the plurality of life, you deny life itself.

II   Religious pluralism

It is useful to recall how pluralization developed within Christianity. The eleventh century saw a split between the Western and Eastern Churches, or, more precisely, the two Churches excommunicated (pronounced *anathemata* against) each other. This reciprocal exclusion led to conflicts and to violence. Then, in the sixteenth century, a conflict developed between proponents of the Reformation and members of the Roman Catholic Church, between two Christian denominations, because both claimed to be state Churches. The eighteenth-century conflict erupted between Christianity and the secular-humanist world in the form of the Enlightenment. Bremer maintains that Europe had not ceased to be multireligious, yet was said to be a Christian continent, which means that Europe was ruled by a Christian exclusivism (indeed by a religious exclusivism) as well as a Christian inclusivism (indeed a religious inclusivism) that served to promote Eurocentrism. Christian exclusivism denies the existence of any truth outside the Church, whereas Christian inclusivism recognizes that aspects of the truth may be present in other religions, but that all those aspects, and their full import, are actually to be found in Christianity. The fact that religious pluralism is present everywhere today in spite of all kinds of resistance is evidence of life's victory over death. The agents of death and the institutions of death cannot destroy life, which survives to reproduce in all its rich variety. The more various life is, the stronger it is.

Reactions to religious pluralism may be positive or negative. Negative reactions are evoked by fear of religious and ideological differences, and by fear of the proponents of other religions and world-views. This fear may become pathological and lead to religious fundamentalism. This deep fear of others, which may be rational or irrational, artificially manufactured or pathological, gives rise to aggression aiming at the annihilation of others, which leads to depression. It also conduces to withdrawal into ourselves, into the ghetto, and into self-isolation. This pathological fear of others leads believers to take refuge in religious collectivism. A religious collective identity, or, more exactly, religious collectivism, is especially evident today in Bosnia-Herzegovina and in the constituent countries of the former Yugoslavia. This is the unanimous finding of our sociologists of religion: Ivan Cvitković, Dino Abazović, Slavica Jakelić, Danijela Majstorović and Duško Trninić.

III   Religion, nationalism, ethnicity

In his book *Konfesija u ratu* (*Denomination and War*), Ivan Cvitković shows how religion has become a kind of national ideology: 'The dominant idea is that of the unity of the denominational and national existence of the nation, and that the nation grows stronger if religion and denomination are strengthened. Religion becomes a kind of national ideology in the process. The national ethos is sacralized ... Religious feast-days have taken on something of the character of national celebrations, which are duly treated in accordance with popular traditions and customs ... Religion and denomination are interpreted as political ideologies, and as the culture from which the nation has emerged. The cultivation of religious awareness has almost completely disappeared as a primary task for religious associations. It has been replaced by the cultivation of the national consciousness.'[3]

In his book *Bosanskohercegovački muslimani između sekularizacije i desekularizacije* (*The Muslims of Bosnia-Herzegovina between Secularization and Desecularization*), Dino Abazović remarks that religion in Bosnia-Herzegovina has entered the service of national politics or nationalism, which he describes as a religious nationalism that makes possible, or gives rise to, a 'religionization' of politics, so that politics is made to serve the religious establishment, and religion is an entitlement to control affairs of state. 'Similarly the existence of a religious nationalism gives rise to an insistence on a symbiosis of the political and religious realms, and on the nationalization of a religious denomination. This precedes the religionization of politics, which itself harks back to a pre-political age when the religious establishment laid claim to affairs of state, since religion was a major (or the most important) element in the construction of the State.'[4]

31

In her book *Kolektivističke religije* (*Collectivist Religions*), Slavica Jakelić uses the term 'collectivist religion' instead of 'religious nationalism' and shows that religion is central to the collective identity in certain post-Communist societies, both symbolically and institutionally. She describes a very close association between religion and the national ideology, the historical and social origins of collectivist Catholicism, and religion and nationalism as two aspects of the collective identity.[5]

In *Diskursi periferije* (*About the Periphery*), Danijela Majstorović writes about the congruence of the religious and ethnic identities, and opines that the term '*vjeroispovijest*' (denominational adherence or religious affiliation) is not wholly appropriate, since it suggests that membership of a religion and a nation at one and the same time includes religiousness, which is not necessarily the case. She thinks that it would be preferable to talk of the accordance of a socio-religious heritage with ethnic identification: 'Among Balkan countries, Bosnia-Herzegovina featured the greatest degree of overlapping of religious and ethnic identity. In that kind of situation it is very difficult to distinguish such closely-related terms both conceptually and psychologically with a great degree of precision. Furthermore, the term '*vjeroispovijest*' (denominational adherence or religious affiliation) itself represents one of the associated terminological difficulties. If denominational adherence or religious affiliation was the overriding criterion, we might say that every Bosnian was a believing Muslim and every Serb a believing Christian belonging to an Orthodox Church, yet there are Bosnians who subscribe to various religions or denominations. The term 'denominational adherence or religious affiliation' is not precise, since it always includes religiousness, which is not necessarily the case in reality. Perhaps it is better to talk of a congruence of socioreligious heritage and ethnic identification, for even if one's ancestors happened to be demonstrably religious, that does not necessarily mean that their children and grandchildren are religious too.[6]

In *Religija pred izazovima globalizacije* (*Religion and the Constraints of Globalization*), Duško Trninić maintains that in the course of globalization nationalism becomes a defence mechanism seeking to protect national sovereignty. Nationalism in conjunction with religion defends the national State, and religion gains a new lease of life by serving the nation: 'In this context religion renews its vitality, because nationalism provides it with an opportunity for its own affirmation, and thus enables it to act as a form of political protest against globalization that helps to defend the national State.'[7]

Membership of a religion and membership of a nation are the two most important forms of adherence in Bosnia-Herzegovina. Anyone who cannot be placed in these two categories may be said to have no identity of classification or as a person. Their membership of their religion and of their nation enables the residents of Bosnia-Herzegovina to consider themselves ontologically, morally, religiously and nationally superior to others. The origins of this presumption, fantasy and arrogance are to be found in pathological fear of others. Presumption and arrogance enmesh them in trauma and hatred, both individual and collective. This kind of hatred leads to the murder of others, to genocide and to suicide. This trauma is handed down from one generation to another and thus becomes a supra-generational phenomenon.

These delusions persuade people that members of other religions and nations are not human beings but filth to be cleaned away. They are convinced that they are getting rid of rubbish, deserve to be acknowledged and rewarded for their efforts, and ought to be hailed as heroes, saviours and beneficiaries of their own people. The two most dangerous modern ideologies to have prevailed in this region (nationalism in the form of Fascism, and Communism in its Stalinist manifestation) banished the freedom of the human individual and raised the collective (established on a national or a social class) to the status of a universal yardstick. In both ideologies the individual became a mere member of the collective. They both replaced love with their particular form of hatred and traduced millions of people in this way. The agents of these ideologies talked of liberating the world from evil, which in the abstract appeared to be a selfless and noble aim. The manipulation peculiar to these systems consisted in locating evil only in members of other nations or of another class, and in seeking to free us from it by murder and carnage. Their hatred was quite boundless and impossible to satisfy. This was shown by the way in which they elevated their (national or class collective) to the status of a false god or idol, in whose name they expressed their hate of their opponents and then annihilated them. The limitless nature of this hatred is also evident from their inability to bring it to an end. Even when they had liquidated all their enemies, their hatred would remain as vital as ever.

IV Nationalism , collectivism, individualism

As for religion, since Christianity had ceased to be a state religion, and accordingly a state ideology, since the French Revolution, it began to serve the nation and therefore the state ideology. Consequently, right up to the present, it has proved difficult to find Christian theologians who have been willing to criticize nationalism openly and without compromise, whereas they have almost all been prepared to criticize Communism. In his latest book, *Hrvati i Crkva* (*The Croats and the Church*), Ivo Banac, a former Professor at Yale now teaching at Zagreb University, relates how the Church was able to avoid the Communist ideology but not nationalism: 'It was much more difficult in the case of the effects of nationalism – the strongest of modern ideologies. In the modern age, the secular mass religion of nationalism managed to plan the cult of the nation at the heart of Christianity.'[8] In this Banac is seconded by the prestigious Bosnian-Herzegovinian historian Dubravko Lovrenović, who maintains that 'The ideology of the nation has found its counterpart in the form of the theology of the nation. The national god was introduced into primal religious ideas and no one, not even the Communists, could dethrone it.'[9] In *Bogozaborav* (*God is Forgotten*), Frano Prcela OP, a Catholic theologian from Zagreb, tells us: 'Religions should never be equated with nations, lest they become mere folk or tribal religions. If the Church takes on a national or ethnic character, it ceases to be catholic, universal. There is no warranty for Catholic ethnocentrism in the Bible and attempts to ground it theologically or give it priestly support are totally impermissible.'[10] Some years ago, our leading theologian, Tomislav Šagi-Bunić, warned us in his article 'Kršćanstvo i nacionalizam' ('Christianity and Nationalism') of the danger of Christianity succumbing to nationalism and betraying its essential nature: 'In the event it is a matter only of a national value, but one that can give rise to fanaticism, since a transcendental value immanent to Christianity per se is wrongly ascribed to it, culminating in a veritable national and human tragedy, and even disaster.'[11] Ivan Bubalo, Professor at the Franciscan College in Sarajevo, writes: 'Nevertheless it is the Church's task to represent the universal values of the Kingdom of God, which rise above everything immanent and partial, and thus above national interests. In this sense it should not submit to politicization or serve the interests of any political cause, and certainly should not enter into any alliance with demagogic advocates of "Realpolitik" in the style of political or ethnic Catholicism.'[12]

On the basis of the foregoing I can confirm that religious collectivism is to the fore among us here in Bosnia-Herzegovina, which means that the collective identity is dominant. People belong to their religious collective, but they have no personal belief, because their individual identity is reduced to the collective identity. Every deviation from collectivism is interpreted as treason. Those who abandon their religion to join another religion or another world-view are traitors worthy only to be treated with disdain. Here there is no normal collective identity but only that extreme version known as the collectivist identity.

Religious individualism is the rule in Western European countries. In this regard the sociologists Grace Davie[13] and Danièle Hervieu-Léger[14] state that militant nationalism has been most unsuccessful in Europe, and that educated Europeans mistrust forms of intense nationalism and religious emotion. Even if they have a distanced relation to organized religion, they will have recourse to it occasionally as the bearer of the collective memory, or because they need comfort when in distress, or require counselling after collective disasters and similar events. Danièle Hervieu-Léger refers to a separation between belief and membership of an organized religion, and Grace Davie describes 'believing without belonging'. People are looking for a new form of religion, because they are searching for answers to their questions about the meaning of their lives, so that their spirituality is in fact a questing spirituality: a personal quest leading to new forms of piety. This gives rise to different relations between various forms of search and the centres of traditional devotion; between those who are firmly set in the traditional form and those who are looking for new forms. Mihail Epstein describes this phase of searching in post-Soviet Russia and uses the term 'minimal religion' in this connection.[15] He calls this religious attitude 'post-atheistic'. In the era of militant atheism all forms of religion were equally subject to repression, so that a certain distance to all religious options was the norm. But this attitude is strictly speaking post-atheistic, since such people developed a sense of God outside religious structures. A certain 'minimal religion' was the form of spirituality experienced within one's own family, among friends, in individuals and in their immediate environment, because the temples of the official religion were too restricted for them. Charles Taylor[16] concludes from this circumstance that a similar situation obtains in 'post-secular' Europe. 'Being spiritual though not religious' is one of the phenomena associated with Epstein's minimal religion in Russia. It is a matter of a spiritual life that keeps a certain distance from the discipline and authority of religious denominations.

It now becomes clear that we are faced with an individualistic rather than a normal, individual identity, and with a collectivist rather than a normal, collective identity. Here we have two extremes that impinge on each other: *extrema tanguntur*. Both of them originate in a pathological fear of others, of what is different and alien, especially of radical difference, of radical strangers, and of absolute strangers. Bernhard Waldenfels[17] describes radical otherness as the kind that a human being considered as an individual cannot evade.

V Fear and aggression

Fear gives rise to aggression against others or leads to being wrapped up in yourself. The individualistic and the collectivist identities see the only authentic form of being as one that conquers and accordingly develops the forms of existence which it encounters. To understand this, we need only recall the European conquests of parts of the rest of the world in modern times. The forms of existence not taken over by Europeans were treated as worthless. But the Europeans turned what was said to be worthless into a form of existence of some value when both the individualistic and collectivist identities refused to acknowledge the alien forms of being which they had not manufactured. Neither of these identities is able to behave morally, because each of them is entirely without any moral awareness and has put paid to ethics. Neither of them is ever guilty of anything, for the other is always the only guilty one. Since others are always blameworthy, and evil is to be found solely in other people, it is justifiable to banish evil by eliminating other people. The individualistic identity negates all its affiliations: national, religious, linguistic and cultural associations, membership of one's own family, its relation to nature, the universe, the human race, and so on. Consequently, this kind of identity is also violent. The collectivist identity reduces individuals to the level of mere members of a collective and simultaneously cancels their existence as free individuals, which makes this kind of identity violent too. Then we realize that the individualistic identity has turned the human ego into an idol, and that the collectivist identity has done the same thing with its collective. This sort of transformation of religion into idolatry is the worst of all perversions.

How can we get rid of the paradigm of fear which gives rise to the individualistic and collectivist identities, that in their turn lead to confrontation with others or to self-isolation? By turning towards the other, and to what is different, new and elusive, because opening up to the other enriches us ontologically. By focussing on others, we become aware of their primacy. In *Thus Spake Zarathustra*, Nietzsche told us that 'You is older than I',[18] and from the beginning of the twentieth century up to now the word 'you' has been the watchword of moral philosophy. Even before Nietzsche, Hegel[19] stressed the importance of the acknowledgement freely uttered by others. A servant's recognition is given under compulsion and is valueless. The only genuine recognition is the fruit of freedom. Buber[20] described the I–you relationship that stands over against the I–it relationship, for 'There is no intrinsic I but only the I of the fundamental I–you and the I of the fundamental I–it.' Max Scheler[21] extended this notion when he remarked that you preceded our I, the other enjoyed primacy, and therefore that taking the you-ness of the other into consideration was the basic category of human thought. Emmanuel Levinas[22] thought that Western thinking and Western freedom virtually negated other-directedness, and cited Abraham as the leading proponent of a philosophy of the other. Nor should we forget that Heidegger[23] in *Being and Time* emphasized the same precedence of the other, as did Karl Rahner[24] in *Hearers of the Word* and Ratzinger[25] in *Introduction to Christianity*. In *Spheres*, Peter Sloterdijk[26] portrays the couple as more authentic than the individual, existence as soaring in a couple with the other person, and humans as 'soaring' or 'suspended' beings.

The primacy of the absolute other is an essential part of all Abrahamitic religions when they recall their origins. Only love of the wholly other and of others can liberate us from our egotism. Only those who are released from the rule of ego (that is, from enslavement by their own selves) can enjoy true freedom of action.

Translated by J. G. Cumming

Notes

1. Christoph Schwöbel, 'Toleranz aus Glauben', in Christoph Schwöbel & Dorothee von Tippelskirch (eds), *Toleranz aus Glauben*, Freiburg im Breisgau, 2002, pp. 11–37.
2. Thomas Bremer, 'Christianity in a Multireligious Europe', *Concilium*, June 2004.
3. Ivan Cvitković, *Konfesija u ratu*, Sarajevo & Zagreb, 2004, pp. 16–17.
4. Dino Abazović, *Bosanskohercegovački muslimani između sekularizacije i desekulariza-cije*, Zagreb & Sarajevo, 2012, p. 107.

5. Slavica Jakelić, *Collectivistic Religions*, Burlington, 2010.
6. Danijela Majstorović, *Diskursi periferije*, Belgrade, 2013, p. 162.
7. Duško Trninić, *Religija pred izazovima globalizacije*, Banja Luka, 2010, p. 79.
8. Ivo Banac, *Hrvati i Crkva*, Zagreb & Sarajevo, 2013, p. 154.
9. Dubravko Lovrenović, 'Bosanskohercegovački Hrvati', Sarajevo, 2 May 2014, p. 33.
10. Frano Prcela, *Bogozaborav*, Zagreb & Sarajevo, 2014, p. 160.
11. Tomislav Šagi-Bunić, 'Kršćanstvo i nacionalizam', Zagreb, 12, 15 June 1969.
12. Ivan Bubalo, *Minima varia*, Rijeka, 2012, p. 236.
13. Grace Davie, *Religion in Britain since 1945: Believing without Belonging*, Oxford, 1994.
14. Danièle Hervieu-Léger, *Le Pélerin et le Converti*, Paris, 1999.
15. Mikhail Epstein, 'Minimal Religion and Post-Atheism: From Apophatic Theology to Minimal Religion', in Mikhail Epstein, Alexander Genis & Slobodanka Vladiv-Glover, *Russian Postmodernism: New Perspectives in Post-Soviet Culture*, New York & Oxford, 1999.
16. Charles Taylor, *A Secular Age*, Cambridge, MA & London, 2007, p. 535.
17. Bernhard Waldenfels, *Topographie des Fremden*, Frankfurt am Main, 1997.
18. Friedrich Nietzsche, *Also sprach Zarathustra*, first complete edition, 1892 (ET: *Thus Spake Zarathrustra*).
19. G. W. F. Hegel, *Phänomenologie des Geistes*, Werke, vol. 3, Frankfurt am Main, 1970, pp. 145–55 (ET: *Phenomenology of Spirit*).
20. Martin Buber, *Ich und Du*, Leipzig, 1923 (ET: *I and Thou*).
21. Max Scheler, *Die Wissensformen und die Gesellschaft*, Leipzig, 1926, p. 53 (ET: *The Forms of Knowledge and Society*).
22. Emmanuel Levinas, *Totalité et Infini: Un essai sur l'extériorité*, Paris, 1961.
23. Martin Heidegger, *Sein und Zeit*, Tübingen, 1972, esp. § 34, p. 163 (ET: *Being and Time*). See also Derrida's comments on this passage in his *Politiques de l'Amitié*, Paris, 1994.
24. Karl Rahner, *Hörer des Wortes*, Munich, 1941 (ET: *Hearers of the Word*).
25. Joseph Ratzinger, *Einführung in das Christentum*, 1988 (ET: *Introduction to Christianity*).
26. Peter Sloterdijk, *Sphären I*, Frankfurt am Main, 1988, p. 488.

Part Two: Identities in the Vortex of Conflict

Living in No-man's-land

REGINA AMMICHT QUINN

'Identity' is a crisis concept, for identities are not simply 'there', but have to be constructed and developed. When crises occur in a context of religion or national politics, identities are often negotiated and interpreted in the light of affiliations. Danis Tanovic, a Bosnian filmmaker (b. 1969), and Hannah Arendt, an American social and political theorist, historian and journalist of German origin and Jewish forebears (1906–75), who identified herself as Jewish, had had personal experiences of national–political and identity crises. Tanovic's narratives show what can happen when people of various identities and affiliations, encounter one another in no-man's-land, between the frontlines of warring forces. We may read Arendt's discursive warning that 'who' someone is must never be obscured or erased by 'what' someone is as a comment on Tanovic's film, although it was expressed 40 years before that film was made. Arendt's dictum that no one has the 'right to obey' can also assist us in forging identities (which also means religious identities) that will not help to foster and perpetuate mortal conflicts.

I Factors of identity

'Identity' is a crisis concept. 'It was a problem from the start, and began as a problem.'[1] We might go so far as to say that if identity were not in a critical state, we would not need it, for then what we are would just be our 'nature'. 'Identity' is in a critical state, because it isn't just 'there'. It has to be constructed, developed and constantly reworked. It can be called in question, denied or revoked. Yet people today treat it as a lifelong concern.

   Until well into the twentieth century, at certain levels of society, biography did not depend on a continual quest for one's own identity but on the three Gs of genealogy, geography and gender, which constituted the setting, limits but also the framework of life. The individual ego is established and marked by setting, limits and framework, and life unfolds between them. Both the way in which we see ourselves and how we are perceived from outside are filtered and controlled through them.

These assumptions are now lost to us in so many important respects. In our situation in life, and in our cultural and geographical location, we have been variously liberated from the bonds of class, vocation, neighbourhood, and partly even family and gender roles. Some people throughout the world have decided to cobble their own identities together as a result.[2] It is as if their societies held do-it-yourself identity shows offering readymade identity kits to be screwed and bolted together in different ways like Meccano, or just glued on like spare parts. Identity crises take other forms in other contexts. In general, however, when external crises break out, especially with regard to religion or national politics, identities are not do-it-yourself products but depend on affiliation. This kind of adherence is insecure. It may be much desired but not guaranteed; it may be enforced yet not desired. The mindset of due affiliation does not tolerate 'mixed' skin colours, ethnicities, nationalities and sexual preferences, and treats ambiguous or vague identities as dangerous. But unambiguous identities are de rigueur.[3]

II Identity and no-man's-land

The conjunction of the critical notion of 'identity' and external crises takes us into a problematical field of study where, for instance, the Bosnian filmmaker Danis Tanovic and the naturalized American, formerly German, social and political thinker, historian and journalist Hannah Arendt can act as guides and advisers (Arendt had Jewish forebears and acknowledged her Jewishness. She was a trained and educated philosopher but refused to call herself one). Danis Tanovic, our first travel guide, leads us into no-man's-land, a critical location of a special kind. In this case the no-man's-land, or disputed ground between the front lines of two opposing armies, is a deserted trench. Although the Bosnian soldier Čiki wears a Rolling Stones tee shirt instead of a conventional uniform, he is battle-hardened, whereas the Serbian soldier Nino, wearing a standard uniform, is an absolute neophyte as far as combat is concerned. They are sitting in this trench as if trapped there. There is another Bosnian soldier, Cera, who is dead, as far as we know. Mining corpses is a known front-line practice, and another, now dead Serbian soldier has placed a mine under him. It is not a contact mine that explodes when someone steps on it but one that goes off when someone takes their weight off it. It will be quite sure to work because it is a quality product 'made in the EU'.

So this special Tanovic-style no-man's-land features an explosive corpse and two young enemies, wounded and desperate. They are both in pain and desperately longing for a smoke. They are both in the same trap. If they leave the trench, someone or other on one side or the other, or both sides at once, will take aim at them. No one lives in no-man's-land or, at least, no one survives there.

Danis Tanovic's *No-man's-land* (2001) is a war film that destroys its own genre.[4] Apart from the first few scenes, whiere there is action and fighting (combat that catapults Čiki and Cera's dead body into the trench), nothing happens. Nothing, at any rate, that we would expect to see in a war film. Or almost nothing. Čiki fires at Nino and doesn't kill him; Nino makes for Čiki with a knife and doesn't kill him. The only thing killed is time. They quarrel. They find out that they have surprising memories in common. Čiki persuades Nino to strip down to his underpants, to clamber out of the trench and signal with a (relatively) white tee shirt, to warn the Bosnian and Serbian units on both sides of their situation, and perhaps prevent them from killing the two soldiers. When nothing happens, they both emerge and wave their white tee shirts. Still with no result.

III   Expectations and events

As the public, as spectators and to some extent as accomplices, we are waiting for something to happen: a reconciliation or an explosion. But neither happens. War, Tanovic shows us, is waiting for Godot, a ridiculous and sad waiting for an outcome that could resolve things or deliver us, but doesn't occur. Of course, something does happen that is beyond the anticipated 'action' of a war film. Three things happen in fact.

The first is that Cera, the apparently dead soldier on the mine, wakes up. He has an itch and just has to scratch himself. He wants to look at his girlfriend's photo, buried in one of his pockets. Since he is alive, he has to piss and shit. But if he moves, they're all doomed. So he lies there unmoving, blinking in the midday sun, behaving as if his body were dead even though he isn't, while Čiki and Nino try to make him halfway comfortable, not only out of common humanity but in their own interest.

The second event is that UN headquarters and the media discover the extraordinary situation in no-man's-land. The UN, inept, incompetent and useless, is asked to help by both sides and is given the opportunity actually to save lives … theoretically, anyway. When he gets the news, the British General realizes from a chess analogy that there are clearly men trapped between the lines, and we realize what kind of collective identiy is ascribed to the collective external actors and their engagement in this war. They are the players. The others are the pieces, which usually means the pawns.

The third event is that Čiki and Nino negotiate their identities. These discussions comprise a perfect five-Act play within a play. In the first Act, both protagonists get rid of their particular signs of identity: their uniforms. They appear in their underclothes and wave their white tee shirts. A Serbian soldier watching this scene through a telescope asks: 'Is he one of us?' And another answers with a shrug: 'You can't tell from the underwear.'

IV Revelations

The second Act shows the two enemies exposed in another way. At some time in the past they both knew the same girl.

You're from Banja Luka, Čiki says to Nino. … I had a girl in Banja Luka once. Sanja.
I knew a Sanja too.
She had … [Čiki models her big breasts]
So did my Sanja.
Blonde.
Yes.
Tall.
Yes.
With a beauty spot.
Yes.
Sanja Čengic! says Čiki excitedly.
I was at school with her, says Nino.
You're kidding?

Cross my heart!
Cera! He knows the Sanja from Banja Luka I told you about!
And we hear Cera's sarcastic reply, somewhat toned down by the fact he's lying on a mine: Yeah, great!

But the first and second Acts don't lead to a third Act of reconciliation. Neither the mutual discarding of uniforms nor shared memories lead to the recognition that both of them are simply young men under the uniforms declaring a national identity, and nothing more than human beings in their naked state of nature. But an ethical interpretation of this kind, which we as spectators would dearly like to believe is true, is too good to be true. For the third Act describes, quite to the contrary, how the 'state of nature' in no-man's-land counts not as a state of shared humanity but as a state of mistrust. Identities, especially identities in no-man's-land, are morally loaded, because identities feed on the particular form of moral superiority.

Čiki and Nino are sitting in one of the dark dugouts in the trench, one of them on the right and the other on the left of a doorway.

Nino: Why on earth did you mess up this beautiful country? Why? Why?
Čiki: What, us?
Nino: Yes!
Čiki: You're nuts! It was you that wanted to separate, not us!
Nino: Because you started the war!
Čiki: You started it!
Nino: What! Who started it?
Čiki both try to ram it home at the same time: You started the war! You started the war!

... until Čiki picks up the gun and aims it at Nino's face: Who started the war?
Silence.
Nino: We started it.
Čiki: Yes, you started it. Stop pissing me off. You're getting on my nerves. Now get out of here. Go on, out!
Čiki forces Nino out of the dugout, then says to himself:
Shit! He's got a nerve to say we started it.

V   Reversal

The fourth Act is a simple reversal of the third Act:

In the meantime, Nino has got hold of the gun. Čiki is about to light a cigarette.

Nino: Give them here!
Čiki changes his mind and throws him the cigarettes. Nino lights up.
Niki: Can I have one?
Nino: No.
Čiki: Why not?
Nino: Because I've got the gun and you haven't … And anyway, who started the war?
Čiki looks away and says nothing.
Nino raises the weapon: Come on! Who started the war?
Čiki: We did.
Cera's voice is heard, still sarcastic: It really doesn't matter, does it, because we're all in the same shit-hole!

In these two mirror scenes, identities are not only constructed by satisfying the claim of moral superiority, but by the power to support this claim. Then we may say not only that the stronger is right because he is stronger, but that the stronger also determines the morality of the case. Religious identities don't come into it.

But that doesn't mean that religion plays no part here. Religion has a non-speaking role in this play and is hidden behind definite words, even though the words definitely spoken express absolute enmity.

The fifth Act of this identity drama shows that it is a tragedy. Čiki and Nino are removed from no-man's-land by UN troops. In an unsupervised moment Čiki picks up a dead man's weapon and shoots Nino, and is himself shot by a UN soldier.

Cera is still there on the mine, not budging.

The UN see themselves as ideal candidates for a heroic role, and fetch a mine expert who is German and precise but can't defuse the mine. We, spectators and accomplices of the UN, are the only ones who know that. The UN authorities think that it would be inappropriate, especially as far as the media are concerned, to become losers instead of heroes. They lie about what is going on, and declare on-camera that some man under a blanket on a stretcher is the soldier saved by the UN alone, and that he is now on his way to hospital, and everyone leaves the scene. Everyone but Cera.

The camera shows the abandoned trench and rises until Cera alone on the mine can be seen from far overhead. Then the screen goes blank and black.

Then there is no longer any possibility of constructing but only of deconstructing an identity.

A no-man's-land is the land in between, a space without possibilities, often empty, deadly, a proverbial or actual dead end. No-man's-land is not only the country that 'belongs' to no one, but the land where there isn't any God and the camera operating as God's eye can retire. Now we the spectators, accomplices like all the rest, can say goodbye to this unbearable image of a man on a mine. We can leave it behind and out of mind.

VI   Illusion and reality

Or, unlike the camera and the eye of God, we can refuse to retire and instead look at and hear the unbearable really happening.

Then Hannah Arendt is our guide. More than 50 years before everyone abandoned Cera on the mine, she experienced her own 'intermediate space', her own no-man's-land.

Hannah Arendt was born in 1906, had to leave Germany in 1933, and was deprived of her German nationality in 1937. Thereupon her identity became that of a pariah, a reject who (as she described in the case of Rahel Varnhagen),[5] as a Jew, remained an outsider in society, which nevertheless gave her access to certain aspects of freedom. Her precarious situation as a German Jew in exile in Paris became acutely dangerous in 1940 after German troops attacking France, the Netherlands and Belgium, occupied Belgium, when the French authorities placed her and other childless women in the Gurs internment camp in the South of France,[6] in a no-man's-land of 'complete hopelessness' packed to overflowing with victims (including 4000 German citizens, mostly Jewish).[7] From 1942 onwards those confined in Gurs were deported to Eastern Europe, and many of them were murdered in the gas-chambers of Auschwitz. Arendt did not share this fate, for she managed to escape with a group of women in 1940 and arrived in New York in 1941.

If we do not wish to abandon and forget Cera on the mine, we need new ways of negotiating and constructing identities. We have to arrange identities in ways that do not end fatally in five Acts, as in Tanovic's play.

In *Vita Activa*[8] (1958–60), Hannah Arendt developed a theory of political action and distinguished between two forms of identity existing in a 'network of associations':[9] 'who' I am and 'what' I am. The 'what' always comes to the fore when we describe people; it may comprise biological attributions, culture or nationality, profession and abilities, and status or its absence. For Arendt, 'who' a person is is revealed in action and speaking.[10] Ultimately, however, the type, outcome and effect of actions are unpredictable. Accordingly, promising and forgiving are the two main characteristics of 'who' I am.[11]

Promising associates us with others' claims, and therefore it is not the 'self' that makes a promise, but the promise that makes the 'self'.[12] Forgiveness takes account of the fact that it is only conditionally possible for us to translate our intentions into actions. Both promise and forgiveness are dependent on each other if a 'who' is to emerge.

VII   Prescribed identity

Arendt tells us that to be a Jew in Nazi Germany meant living in a political present that 'had dicated a form of adherence in which the very question of personal identity was also decided along the lines of anonymity, namelessness'.[13] In a situation like that 'what' a human being is – Jewish, alien, inferior – is laid down, preordained, 'dictated', and then ultimately the 'who' is replaced by the 'what'. The promise that I give to others and need from others, and the forgiveness that I need from others and give to others, disappear behind 'what' I am. This 'what' can easily be used for exclusion, or for execution.

Although our environments and situations are clearly different from Arendt's environments and situations in the 1930s and 1940s, people today constantly violently substitute a 'what' for 'who'. At the same time, however, there are many situations in which this reduction of 'who' to 'what' can be freely chosen rather than violently exacted. Uncomplainingly accepting a 'what' always promises an easy or easier life. Wherever people readily and assiduously agree, limit and adapt themselves to 'what', authorities gain power over these identities. Others use power to decide which forms of 'what' are appropriate, 'good' and germane, and which forms of 'what' are inappropriate, wrong and to be discarded. If there are real or supposed internal or external conflicts, crises or threats in a society, there is an increasing danger that those with power will use that power to define the 'what' of human beings. This is an opportunity to make clear 'what' someone 'really' is and how we can defend ourselves from others who are not that.

These 'what' identities, a variation on the 'authoritarian character',[14] have a great potential for generating conflicts, while these conflicts for their part give rise to identities of that kind.

VIII   Obedience and identity

'No one has ... the right to obey.'[15] This extraordinary moral assertion is to be understood in the context of Arendt's controversial work on SS Lieutenant-Colonel Adolf Eichmann, head of the Gestapo Department for Jewish Affairs, who played the leading role in the deportation for extermination by the Germans of at least three million Jews in the Shoah, or Holocaust. During his trial in Jerusalem, Eichmann explained his own moral code and tried to make it plain how he saw himself as following the philosopher Kant – at least up to a certain point: as a good, law-abiding citizen doing his duty.[16]

Arendt's dictum, which can certainly apply beyond her own direct intention, does not mean that no one should obey, or that no one must obey. The dictum means that no one has the right to obey. Arendt assumes that there are people who want to be bound by a right to obey. This seems quite paradoxical, for they want to have to do something.

This paradox still and always makes entire sense in everyday life. Obedience saves time, and dispenses us from worries, controversies, sleepless nights and too much thinking. Furthermore, obedience can bring us privileges such as our parents' pride, teachers' praise, acceptance by generals, the indifferences of dictators, and God's love.

Yet Hannah Arendt maintains instead that no one has the right to earn privileges by obedience. Not even those who are intent on obtaining the reward of God's love. If identities are based on this profound conviction of a right to obey, they are dangerous: for themselves and for others.

Religious identities are particularly subject to these claims to a privileged right to obey, especially if they are interwoven with national foundation myths and identity politics. If religion prizes the 'what'-I-am

49

identity more highly than a 'who'-I-am identity, it becomes an institution of sheer adherence, and faith retreats into the background. Promising and forgiving no longer have any part to play. Instead, redoubtable mechanisms of inclusion and exclusion are established within which people grow used to wanting to obey, and finally to demanding a right to obey. If religious authorities and communities fail to resist these tendencies, all they do is dig new trenches, keep the old ones going, and produce an never-ending line of no-man's-lands that are no-go areas for God as well as fatal for humans.

Then, we might say, Hannah Arendt takes us back to the trench where Cera is still and for ever lying on his mine. Cera on the mine, dead still and abandoned by everyone, shows how the unending, timeless, deathly system works.

We spectators and complices have the task of ending this system of 'what'-I-am identities. That enables us to set the image of Cera on the mine in the symbolic landscape of no-man's-land in our own era and in our own particular space, so that it becomes a yardstick for us now. A yardstick of this kind prompts us to ask which identities our present surroundings give rise to; where a 'right to obey' is called for; what kind of promises and forgiveness we supply, and thus constitute an identity; and where the boundaries between revenge and justice are to be found.

For the Church and its task of supporting and forming religious identities, this means that religious identities that are not 'who'-I-am but 'what'-I-am identities, traduce not only faith but the faithful. Religious identities especially show that 'promising' and 'forgiving' are fundamental actions that build and form identities.

There should be no room for a 'right to obey' here. Only if the Church is constructed with, and constantly changed by, 'who' identities, will it be able to monitor its own symbolic landscape continually, and thus transform not only the dangerous, inimical and desperate no-man's-land, but its very own self. It is too late for Cera, though perhaps not for us.

Translated by J. G. Cumming

Notes

1. Zygmund Bauman, 'Schwache Staaten. Globalisierung und die Spaltung der Gesellschaft', in Ulrich Beck (ed.), *Kinder der Freiheit*, Frankfurt am Main, 1997, pp. 315–32, 134.
2. *Cf.* in this regard (with an appropriate coinage) Peter Gross, 'Bastelmentalität – ein "postmoderner" Schwebezustand?', in Thomas Schmid (ed.), *Das pfeifende Schwein*,

Berlin, 1985, pp. 63–84. See also Rolf Eickelpasch & Claudia Rademacher, *Identität*, Bielefeld, 3rd ed., 2004.
3. Amin Malouf, *In the Name of Identity: Violence and the Need to Belong*, New York, 2012; Amartya Sen, *Identity and Violence*, Harmondsworth & New York, 2006.
4. *Cf.* Amy Cobin, 'No Man's Land', *Film Quarterly*, Autumn 2006, vol. 60:1, accessed at http://www.filmquarterly.org/2006/09/no-mans-land/.
5. Hannah Arendt, *Rahel Varnhagen: Lebensgeschichte einer deutschen Jüdin aus der Romantik*, Munich, 1959, 10th ed., 2003; ET.: *Rahel Varnhagen: The Life of a Jewish Woman*, rev. ed., New York, 1974.
6. At this point some 20,000 people were housed in a total of 400 barracks. In each case up to 60 individuals shared one of the 25 m² barracks, which were equipped neither with water nor with toilets.
7. Susi Eisenberg-Bach, quoted in *Gurs – ein Internierungslager in Südfrankreich 1939–43: Literarische Zeugnisse, Briefe, Berichte*, Hamburg, 1991, p. 21; *cf.* Maria Krehbiel-Darmstaedter, *Briefe aus Gurs und Limonest 1940–1943*, Heidelberg, 1970. See also Alois Prinz, *Beruf Philosophin oder Die Liebe zur Welt: Die Lebensgeschichte der Hannah Arendt*, Weinheim & Basle, 1998, pp. 94–107.
8. Hannah Arendt, *Vita activa oder Vom tätigen Leben*, Munich, 1981; *The Human Condition*, 2nd ed., Chicago & London, 1998.
9. Tobias Matzner, *Vita Variabilis: Handelnde und ihre Welt nach Hannah Arendt und Ludwig Wittgenstein*, Würzburg, 2013, p. 193.
10. H. Arendt, *Vita activa ...*, *op. cit.*, pp. 167ff.
11. *Ibid.*, pp. 231–43.
12. 'Not the self makes the promise but the promise makes the self.' Lisa Jane Disch, *Hannah Arendt and the Limits of Philosophy*, Ithaca & London, 1996, p. 52. Quoted by T. Matzner, *op. cit.*, p. 169.
13. Hannah Arendt, *Menschen in finsteren Zeiten*, Munich, 1989, p. 34; Eng. tr., *Men in Dark Times*, New York, 1968.
14. Theodor W. Adorno, *Studien zum autoritären Charakter*, Frankfurt, 1995; T. W. Adorno, E. Frenkel-Brunswik *et al.*, *The Authoritarian Personality*, New York, 1950; Erich Fromm, Max Horkheimer *et al.*, *Studien über Autorität und Familie*, 2 vols, Lüneburg, 1936; Wilhelm Reich, *Die Massenpsychologie des Faschismus*, 1933; 2nd rev. ed., Cologne, 1971; ET: *The Mass Psychology of Fascism*, New York, 1971.
15. Hannah Arendt & Joachim Fest, *Eichmann war von empörender Dummheit: Gespräche und Briefe*, Ursula Ludz & Thomas Wild (eds), Munich, 2011, p. 44.
16. Hannah Arendt, *Eichmann in Jerusalem: A Report on the Banality of Evil*, New York, 1963; Ger. version: *Eichmann in Jerusalem: Ein Bericht von der Banalität des Bösen*, Munich, 1964, new ed., 1986, pp. 174–89.

Empires, Wars and Survival in Bosnia and Herzegovina

UGO VLAISAVLJEVIĆ

There are three major Bosnian ethnic communities, because at least three past empires had such a strong influence on the local population that the acculturation they exercised in the past has come to determine the fate of large numbers of people today. Each community has its own privileged imperial reference, and simultaneously excludes the similar references of neighbouring communities. They are different because their choice of constitutive imperial culture is not the same. What one Bosnian community sees as a very positive imperial influence, and adopts as a crucial identity marker, becomes a perilous negative influence to be rejected by the other two communities.

I Introduction

The prerequisites for the formation of an ethnic community are not only (a) the existence of a social group whose members exhibit a pronounced sense of solidarity (that is, a community that perfectly fits the standard definition); and (b) the presence of common cultural features that are characteristic only of this community, shared by all its members, and liable to be handed on as a common cultural heritage; but (c) the firm conviction that all members of the community are related by ties of kinship. The first two are sufficient conditions, whereas the third is a necessary condition. Although it is not difficult to show that this belief is illusory with regard to any particular community, that does not mean that the community in question is wholly imaginary, and that its shared features are fictional.

What kind of relationship are we dealing with here? If we assume that the question is academically serious in some way, we might say that we are faced with a very distant form of kinship based on conjectural and extremely tenuous filaments of relationship, that are nevertheless conceived of as a very firm network of intimate intrafamilial relations, primarily in the forms of fraternity and sonship. Of course, it is impossible to maintain a relationship claimed by an entire nation, unless it is transmitted by a specific cultural model. The cultural model secures kin relationships of this kind and makes them possible. Ethnology has shown that natural links are not merely to be sought in the original basic forms of kinship, but that this kind of 'natural relationship' relies on a great number of symbolic models provided by various cultural forms.[1]

Ethnic relations cannot be maintained without a cultural form, that is, without what is known as ethnic culture, but this form is not equivalent to kinship. Kinship is not a mere effect produced by a cultural form and then pemanently incorporated in the consciousness of a specific human group.

II Imperial rule and acculturation

In this part of the world, there has been no lack of profound transformations of ethnic identity, and they are to be read exclusively as the outcome of gradual, protracted changes that came with the struggle to retain a cultural heritage under the domination of great empires that kept local ethnic communities under their cultural, political, state and so on tutelage for centuries.[2] 'Antagonistic acculturation' turned out to be the most important survival strategy in this situation of symbolic incorporation.[3] Although it was impossible to escape the overwhelmingly powerful alien influence, complete surrender to it was unthinkable. Since the general situation was a fight for survival in a symbolic universe, acquisition of the alien cultural matter might prove so exhaustive that in the end there was almost nothing left of the original form of culture of the dominated ethnic community. Nevertheless, sheer survival demanded that a sufficient number of admittedly distorted, yet still distinctive or antagonistically composed, cultural features were retained to ensure that this cultural community remained different enough to appear distinct from the community in which it immersed itself in order to carry on living at all.

We might say that the local ethnic communities, which were subjected to centuries-long wars of annihilation and the loss of 'soul' in times of peace, were well rehearsed in strategies to ensure survival. Nevertheless, we have to avoid the danger of falling for a retrospective illusion. It is possible that we can equate these strategies with ethnopolitics only with the dawn of the modern era.

During the thousand years of imperial conquests and of incorporation of local communities in alien state orders and cultures, the acculturation processes to which these ethnic communities were exposed for so long have left deep traces in their collective selfhood or characteristic cultural forms, whether this acculturation became antagonistic or not. An ethnic community can withstand the temptations of a powerful and long-lasting acculturation by resorting to defensive isolation, which is the ultimate form of resistance. But it can also survive as a community, irrespective of the desire of most of its members to be assimilated by the dominant culture.[4] It is characteristic of local ethnic communities that each of them should look back to a past imperial culture to which it feels especially indebted for the shaping of its own ethnocultural identity. This privileged relationship is essentially a later form of reference that requires the existence of a post-imperial state of affairs, in which the effects of acculturation support the strategies of an antagonistic acculturation in an inimical encounter with other, up-to-date cultural influences that threaten the survival of this ethnic community.[5]

Irrespective of how a to some extent long-lasting alien order, usually in the imperial mould, was accepted by the particular local ethnic community, it could not help but deeply mark the genealogy of the identities of the affected communities. During the process of penetration by powerful alien overlords, until their departure in the present era, as long as that process lasted at least a few centuries, significant changes took place in ethnic selfhood that have proved to be as impressive and ineradicable as a tree trunk's annual rings.

III   A faith community as a group of related individuals

We know for certain that in the past of Bosnia and Herzegovina religious adherence brought certain people together and decided that they would be subjected to a specific fate. That was not only the fate of belonging to a faith community, but that of adherence to an ethnic community. This fate is ethnic and not merely religious, since the community of believers exposed to the rigours and temptations of history (with facing the threat of extinction heading the list), emerged from the experience as a group of related individuals. In this respect, special emphasis should be laid on the difference between ethnic and religious, even though it is quite subtle: the three nations which have been called recently the 'three constitutive peoples of Bosnia and Herzegovina', because they survived all the vagaries of fate as ethnic groups for centuries, were mainly condemned to suffer this fate as faith communities.

Perseverance in one faith, from one generation to another, and from one century to another, meant that certain groups experienced a quite specific fate precisely as faith communities. An ethnic transformation of denominational affiliation is possible only if orientation to a faith for generations allows the survival of an ethnic community, when the group in question is equally exposed to the danger of extinction. By firmly adopting a specific faith, a community also exposes itself to mortal danger or is allowed to hope that it will survive indefinitely.

For a religion to serve as the basis on which to construct an ethnic identity, in order to function as an ethnic culture, that is, as a separate cultural form with which the destiny of collective life is associated, religion 'pure and simple' has to take the form of a partial religion, one religion among several, and must be thought to contain much more than the mere profession and practice of belief. This means that religion has to exist as a culture, as a system of values and pattern of behaviour, and even indeed as a state and political order. In past centuries, these two conditions were fulfilled in an exemplary fashion in Bosnia and Herzegovina: (a) three survival communities evolved alongside the three monotheistic religions, so that each (universalist and monotheistic) religion received its partial form (as 'ours' over against the 'others'); (b) all three religions were 'imported' by acts of imperial conquest, and had to prove themselves for centuries as specific cultures, systems of state order, and spiritual worlds of alien powers that ruled the earthly life of the world and determined its fate.

The nature of the ethnic identity of a community is only fully comprehensible if we take its relation to significant others into consideration. In the present context, the significant others are the neighbours, and primarily the immediate neighbours: other ethnic communities. But they are also powerful intruders: the imperial conquerors who settled in this part of the world for a long period of time, and were thereby enmeshed in (fateful) constitutive interethnic relations. It was religion precisely that exerted such a strong influence on the type of relations experienced by the communities among themselves, which resisted the ups and downs of imperial presence.[6] Three communities, those of Catholics, Orthodox and Muslims, proved to be the largest and most persistent. But the distant foreigners, who penetrated thus far into the immediate neighbourhood with sword and shield, also entered the sphere of local communal life as ethnic communities defined by faith.

The situation and fate of the local population in every new imperial order were decided by its faith. The three religions had different valences and capacities for interweaving with the religious and political culture of the newcomers. They might be incompatible or compatible with them to a greater or lesser extent. With a change in imperial regime, the community on which fate had smiled up to that point might find itself facing all the cruelty of a new power. These fateful interreligious relations among the longtime residents themselves, but also those with the alien newcomers, relations, that is, that united communities with regard to their collective identities, resulted in their experiencing their commonality as an ethnic bond. The very fact that there was no other form of commonality that lasted for centuries, and was inscribed as it were in networks of filiation, indicates its ethnic nature.

IV The situation in Bosnia and Herzegovina

When analyzing the historical constitution of ethnic communities in Bosnia and Herzegovina, it is essential to note how the denomination was inscribed in the group genealogy. As the etymology of the word genealogy shows, a kind of textbook, or a description handed down from one generation to another, is needed for instruction in family relations, and to read and interpret the genealogical table or pedigree. If a religious affiliation has been transformed into an ethnic affiliation (or an ethnic affiliation into a religious affiliation), distinct features of one must simultaneously represent the features of the other adherence. Since there is no individual ethnic existence without the assignation of an ethnic name, it is assumed that Islam, Catholicism and Orthodoxy offer this sort of guide for genealogical researchers. Bosnians, Croats and Serbs form three ethnic communities, which have survived for centuries as related groups, mainly because the adherence of each individual to his or her community could be indicated by means of the proper name, which applied in the case of both first names and family names.

The three ethnic communities exist as three families of proper names in a symbolic space which is decisive for filiation.[7] These three groups of ethnic designations, which were handed down from older to younger generations, from the dead to the living, were taken from the semiotic treasuries of sacred texts and imperial cultures, which were characterized by these sacred texts. If we meet strangers, we know immediately from their names which community they belong to: for that is generally a reliably distinctive marker of their collective identity (if the evidence is uncertain, then the addition of the father's name is usually all that is needed to settle the matter). If his name leads us to its location in in the distribution of different groups of names, when the family name is the most trustworthy indication of an individual's genealogical background, we find that this point is also the interface of denomination and ethnic kinship. Details of proper names indicate a location where a Catholic and a Croat, a Muslim and a Bosnian, a Serb and an Orthodox Christian represent one and the same community identity. Admittedly, this duality of essential characteristics of identification leaves scarcely any room for individual choice, for recording the specific identity of an individual in a genealogy. Is it possible to be a Catholic but not a Croat, a Muslim but not a Bosnian, an Orthodox Christian but not a Serb? And of course: a Croat but not a Catholic, a Muslim but not a Bosnian, an Orthodox Christian but not a Serb? In some way, admittedly, you can be all of these, yet the different collective fates of the individual major communities of Bosnia and Herzegovina have enforced and fixed this kind of linkage, so that in comparison all other constructions of common and individual forms of identity are exceptions and deviations, and are seen as ways of shrinking the community.

But since the connection between what is religious and what is ethnic occurs by way of genealogy, belonging to ethnic communities of this kind does not presuppose that members have actually to practise the religion in question as worhsippers and so on, yet the characteristic of ethnic identity indicates that an ancestor was a believer (and practised precisely the faith on the basis of which the relevant ethnic identity was constructed), and that this forebear fatefully inscribed his religious affiliation permanently in the names of his own descendant. Since, in the case of all three communities, religion is a cultural form of ethnic identity and the most important emblem of ethnic culture, the call to practise the religion of one's own ancestors is both a summons to preserve and maintain one's own ethnic identity and to acknowledge one's bond with one's own community and its cultural heritage. The return of religion in recent years is indeed characterized by appeals of this kind, and by public reproaches that a lack of religion is a sign of an individual's alienation and moral turpitude.

V Identity by descent

A major phenomenon that occurs as a result of this agreement of the ethnic and the denominational is a certain transmission of the ancestral faith to descendants. When religion is registered in the networks of filiation, this means that it can be deactivated and reactivated, as long as the ethnic identity persists. A descendant who loses his faith and becomes an unbeliever does not lose just any faith, but the very faith that has been handed down to him by way of family relationships. It can easily be seen that during a fairly long stretch of time, such as the period spent under the sway of militant atheism during the Tito regime, it was even possible for several generations to 'abandon' their faith. But, if they persist, the continuity of family names enables the genealogical networks to bypass any such individual tendency and treat it as a kind of temporary stalling of the system. Neither the ethnic nor the denominational connection with one's forebears has disappeared completely when these genealogical links prove faulty and come to a standstill. After all, there is still a guarantee that a descendant can reactivate his or her twofold affiliation in the future, and return to the true faith. It is possible that only conversion to another faith could cut the threads of ethnic kinship and lead to a new berth, as it were, in the other community that is ethnically related to his or her new religion. In any case, an effect of this kind is possible only if the change of faith affects the characteristics of ethnic affiliation and the naming of the convert's descendants. Therefore, a change of faith is the cardinal sin in a local context, because it is seen as a sign of apostasy and of treason to one's own community or, even worse, to one's one kin.

We usually refer to the three ethnic communities of Catholics, Muslims and Orthodox. In the local situation the use of an initial capital letter betrays the ethnicization of religious affiliation.[8] Surely that means that we take into account the historical fate of only one ethnic community, the Bosnian, as the model of an ethnically constituted community, although we called Bosnians 'Muslims' in the written language until not so long ago. Surely the constitutive nature of the other two communities shows that we must see the process by which a dominant collective identity is constructed in reverse, following, that is, the reception process of a religion from the starting-point of ethnic identity, and as a subsequent, derived acquisition of identity. Compared with the Serbs and Croats, the Bosnians would seem to have acquired their ethnic names as replacements for their denominational names only much later, in the very recent past in fact. But does that really prove that the ethnic is more advantageous than the denominational in the historic development of common features of local communities? It is not difficult to show that the assumption of ethnic names among the Serbs and Croats occurred only at a similarly late date, as the result of a very late awakening (in the nineteenth century) of a national self-awareness under the influence of modern ideologies. Even if we were to confirm that this conjunction occurred at a much earlier date, then it would evidently accord with the 'rule of faith':[9] it was the Orthodox Christians who came to think of themselves as Serbs, and the Catholics who saw themselves as Croats. Even if Muslims believed for the space of several generations that they were Serbs or Croats of the Muslim faith, that would not signify the precedence (of a pure) ethnic identity over the denominational identity. Once again, that could have been the result of a subsequent dethnicization of denominational affiliation, or of a tenacious memory of some forebear who was a believing Christian.

It is certain that none of the three communities lags behind in constituting its own ethnic identity. For centuries already, all three have enjoyed a secure form of filiation on the basis of the repository of a clearly separate and formed family of ethnonyms (or ethnic names for peoples, nations or groups). Accordingly, their common characteristics are continually reconstructed as kinship. We know a priori that their kinship can be secured only by a lasting incorporation of the community in the protective membrane of a 'complex of myth and symbolism'. Religious cultures act as historically effective forms of this kind, so that ethnic communities come down to us as Catholics, Muslims and Orthodox from the instability of the past, and by way of the networks of communitarian genealogy. At all events, considered in isolation, the ethnic kinship which some ethno-politicans consider to be beyond any need of proof, nourishes the conviction that the community exists as such, quite apart from any cultural form and in spite of all historical changes, as something like a 'natural aboriginal identity'.

But whenever we try to separate ethnicity from religion, that is, from the cultural form which religion confers on it, it is impossible to find a sufficiently reliable substitute. Then the presence of a collective biological body of an ethnic group is taken as reality, an assumption which is not free from a form of justification based explicitly or implicitly on a racial theory of some kind. The need to seek the intervention of racial theory shows how impossible it is for an ethnic entity to survive in a pure and simple form for centuries and then subsequently to derive from a specific ethnic culture. If there had been an original self-sufficient form of ethnic existence in this location, a community, that is, based on kinship, that pre-existent form would have been deconstructed by the religious culture, which would have bonded it closely to itself, and done so in the form of an imperial culture.

VI Conclusion

Consequently, every local ethnic culture is deconstructed and in no case monolithic, but rather like a fan made up of different cultural contents held together by a particular cultural form.The cultural memory of every ethnic community bears layers of different enthnic cultures which are actually deposits of former imperial systems. This means that each one of them offers its members several models of ethnic personality. Although these models can be arranged in groups, that does not mean that they do not coincide, at least in part.

These communities are distinguished from one another primarily as faith communities, although their ethnic character allows their link with religion to remain entirely virtual or 'frozen'. As far as the importance of ethnic culture for ethnic identity is concerned, it is more appropriate to speak here of long-preserved or newly revived remnants of former imperial orders, which at one time the overwhelming force of acculturation under the aegis of this or that religion compelled the local population to accept.

In any case, as already deduced, a community considered as a ethnic community for that very reason acknowledges that, in the necessity of its struggle for survival, it is basically capable of freeing itself from its dominant cultural form. This means that if a community has been ethnicized, especially as a faith community, it can surivive the loss of its religion, on condition that it is in a position to retain its ethnic names. The Bosnians would be just as unlikely as the Croats and Serbs to disappear as a(n ethnic) community, if under certain conditions their community were to become largely unbelieving, because it would have retained the kin relationship even if the name had been relinquished. But that very same nominal relationship would maintain Islam, Catholicism and Orthodoxy even for generations as a kind of registration as religion for subsequent reactivation. On the other hand, in order to register the lineage for the future in the genealogical tables of an ethnic group, it is necessary to remain loyal to the religious foundations of its culture. A disciplined use of the ethnic register of names, of the general rules whereby names are allocated to members of the community, is inconceivable apart from the ethnic culture referred to by those names.

Translated by J. G. Cumming

Notes

1. Claude Lévi-Strauss, *Les Structures élémentaires de la parenté*, The Hague, 1967; ET: *The Elementary Structures of Kinship*, ed. Rodney Needham, London & New York, 1969. One might very crudely summarize the innovatory views of this French ethnologist on kinship by saying that he revealed the primary logical structures beneath relationships, and showed how in all human societies a biological relation leads to a social relation defining and controlling a group. *Cf.* Marcel Hénaff, *Claude Lévi-Strauss et l'anthropologie structurale*, Paris, 1991, p. 146.
2. Although a surprise campaign by powerful armed forces might threaten a local ethnic community with the grim fate of its complete eradication, the gradual and unremarked loss of the most important features of its ethnic culture (by acculturation) in long-lasting periods of peace under alien rule was not necessarily a more welcome fate. Just as extermination is the greatest danger threatening small nations in time of war, so acculturation and assimilation are the fates they must fear most of all in times of peace.
3. *Cf.* George Devereux & Edwin M. Loeb, 'Antagonistic Acculturation', *American Sociological Review* 8, April 1943, pp. 133–47.
4. *Cf.* Raymond H. C. Teske Jr & Bardin H. Nelson, 'Acculturation and Assimilation: A Clarification', *American Ethnologist* 1: 2 (1974), pp. 351–67.
5. U. Vlaisavljević, 'La constitution guerrière des petites nations des Balkans ou "Qui s'agit-il de réconcilier en Bosnie-Herzégovine?"' / 'The War Constitution of the Small Nations of the Balkans, or "Who is to be reconciled in Bosnia and Herzegovina?"', *Transeuropéennes*, Paris, 14/15, pp. 125–41.
6. This metaphor was adopted by Michael Walzer, who used it to refer to the major role played by a foreign imperial regime in the development of the collective identity of certain nations. See also *On Toleration*, New Haven & London, 1997, pp. 14 ff.
7. Ugo Vlaisavljević, 'Trois langues ou trois familles de noms propres d'une même langue?', in Christiane Montécot, Vladimir Osipov & Sophie Vassilako (eds), *Autour du nom propre* (Cahiers balkaniques 32), Paris, 2001, pp. 193–208.
8. In Bosnian and Serbo-Croat religious designations are given lower-case initial letters. When the Bosnian Muslims were recognized as an ethnic group in their own right, the denominational designation received an initial capital, as is usual for one's ethnic affiliation.
9. See also Banac, 'Vjersko pravilo i dubrovačka iznimka: geneza dubrovačkog kruga Srba katolika', *Raspad Jugoslavije*, Zagreb, 2001, pp. 67–80.

Identity, Tension and Conflict

DŽEVAD KARAHASAN

In this article I borrow terms and concepts from dramaturgy to examine notions of identity, as well as the lines of demarcation and the relations between identities. A basic distinction in dramaturgy is that drawn between conflict and tension. Tension is a complex phenomenon consisting of at least two correlates, a specific pool of common and associative features between the correlates, and a corresponding group of differences between the correlates and their desires, needs and intentions. Conflict, however, is a simple relation in which the identities that have existed in a tense relation are reduced to no more than a single dimension, and to a relation in which 'I' is simply 'not you'. The second essential aspect of the article is the conviction that a rationalistic approach using univocal and one-dimensional identities and relations can neither enable us to understand nor help us to describe complex identities and relations, such as individual human identities and the relations between such identities. Depending on their degree of complexity, cultural identities are close or equivalent to individual human identities. Consequently, any attempt to consider cultural identities using the methods and instruments of mechanical and mathematical thought leads to simplifications and distorts the objects under consideration.

I   Nature and limits

Identity is inseparably associated with boundary; logically it is also produced when an entity delineates itself and thereby receives a form that distinguishes it from everything else. Consequently, identity and boundary are reciprocally determinative, to such an extent that it is impossible to understand the one if the other is left out of consideration. The boundary of an entity is directly dependent on its nature, and our understanding of boundary will determine how we understand its delineation. At least, that is how it will be apprehended by any approach that adapts its methods and tools to the nature of that which it wishes to conceive.

The limits of my essential being are the form of my identity, we might say, paraphrasing Wittgenstein ('It is self-evident that identity is not a relation between objects.' etc., *Tractatus Logico-Philosophicus*). But where are the limits of my being? Let us say that the skin is the boundary of my body and that my corporeal self finds its limit in my skin, which separates me from everything else: that is, from everything that is not-myself, not-I. But I fear that no one would agree with this who has touched another person in an access of love, longing or loathing. They know that the skin also discloses other people to us, and that this is the only way in which we can acknowledge what we recognize about other people by touching them. The skin, then, is a boundary that separates and joins, closes off and opens up. If my skin becomes a boundary that only separates and closes off, I shall possibly continue in that state, but then I shall certainly no longer be alive. Then I shall also be deprived of the breath by means of which I now connect with the world, and through which the outside world (the world of not-I) enters me. Yes, then, when I am dead, the skin is indeed the end of my body and the boundary separating me from everything, but as long as I am alive it is not and cannot be that. This shows how inadequately what is probably the most widespread current notion of boundary (that according to which the boundary brings to an end and closes off what it bounds) says about a living creature and its identity. This kind of boundary applies in geometry, in mechanics, and to dead objects. The sides of a triangle are its boundaries and its end. Everything that lies beyond these sides is the not-I of the triangle in question. If this triangle impinges on a square and shares a side with it, this side clearly and unequivocally represents the border separating two geometrical forms. The case of mechanically closed things is similar. The place where this table ends forms its boundary, from which point onwards something quite distinct begins, even if that quite distinct thing is also a table entirely like the first one.

The situation of living beings is not and cannot be like that. Imagine a tree whose bark, and especially the casing of its roots, was the boundary separating it from everything else. We would certainly all agree that this tree could not live long. An entity lives as long as it is open and somehow connected with the infinite ocean of life. Therefore, the mechanical type of boundary does not help us to understand the identity of a living creature that is not one-dimensional and defined in the same way as the identities of mathematical and mechanical phenomena. Nor is the mechanical or mathematical 'either-or' logic any more useful in this context. This form is a triangle or it is not a triangle, and its side clearly and unequivocally demarcates this form from everything that it is not. Accordingly, the boundary determines the geometrical figure negatively as distinguished from everything that is not the figure itself. This is also the case with mechanically closed things. The identity of this table is produced by its negative determination as distinguished from everything that is not this table.

Translated into the terminology of dramaturgy, this would mean that the identity of mathematical and mechanical phenomena is produced by conflict, and the identity of living things by the tense relationship to the not-I of the phenomenon in question. The triangle is that which it is because it is not an angle, not a square and not an octagon, just as this table is that which it is because it is not a chair, not a cupboard, and not any other table, and not an oak, not a fish, and so on. If one of these phenomena has something in common with another phenomenon, this possession of a common feature does not call its finality in question. Its boundary ends it, closes it off, and isolates it from everything that it not that phenomenon itself. I said that a living creature would cease to be alive if it, that is, if its identity were produced in this way. It is not determined negatively in relation to its not-I, but stands in a tense relationship to it. Tension is a relationship in which the correlates have a specific amount in common, and just as much or even more of what distinguishes them from each other. What they have in common is the basis of exchange and understanding between the correlates, whereas that which distinguishes them from each other does not allow the identities of the correlates to be ignored, confused or forgotten.

II Dramatic tension

Tension, for instance, is a relationship in which the characters in a well-written drama are placed over against one another. Oedipus and Teiresias, protagonists of Sophocles' tragedy *Oedipus Tyrannus* (*King Oedipus*), have a lot in common. They are both uncompromising seekers after truth, and they are both 'chosen' beings, marked out both because of their social reputation and because of the knowledge they possess. They are both high-ranking individuals who are expected to furnish solutions, and they both embody authority. But there are many things that distinguish them from one another and prevent them from agreeing. Teiresias is a priest, and Oedipus is King of Thebes; Teiresias is blind, and the shrewd Oedipus can see well; Teiresias is a lonely man who lives in isolation, and Oedipus is a ruler who surrounds himself with people and enjoys the respect they pay him. The feature that separates them most of all is the type of knowledge which they have received. Teiresias is inspired, and he possesses sacred knowledge about matters concealed from the physical eyes of human beings (and therefore he is blind, like Homer, as Faust will be at the end of Goethe's tragedy, and as Oedipus himself will be eventually), whereas Oedipus is a perceptive observer who knows as much as can be known with the human mind and powers of observation. But that is all he does and can know, and therefore his fate and his own essential nature are hidden from him. His identity is unknown to him, we would say nowadays, because it is impossible to know the human identity by external observation, and to express it in terms of facts; that is, it cannot be reduced to facts. The relation between what they have in common and what distinguishes them from one another makes their *agon* (the 'discussion,' or, that is, the confrontation between them) inevitable whenever they are in the same place at the same time. The drama depends on this juxtaposition, as it were.

In its concern to attain to the univocality of mathematical and mechanical relations in all instances, the rationalistic (Oedipal?) one-sidedness of modern culture treats the tense relationship of the two protagonists as a conflict, and their agon not as discussion and juxtaposition, but as a clash or collision. The rationalistic approach does not discern (is not capable of discerning?) the obvious reciprocal dependence of the figures (identities) of Oedipus and Teiresias, which is so emphatic that we may certainly say that they condition, display, and make each other conceivable. The differences between them derive their significance and sense from what they have in common, and what is common to them makes their juxtaposition and discussion between them inevitable, because that makes the differences especially weighty. We can recognize and even make out Oedipus's rationalism only in direct relation to the sacred knowledge of the prophet Teiresias, just as we can neither see nor recognize Teiresias' knowledge of hidden things without the active relationship of the two Sophoclean protagonists. Without the confident and literally aggressive action of

Oedipus, Teiresias would not have uttered what he knows and sees with his inner eye, because he, who knows fate, also knows that the inevitable should not be uttered. Moreover, without the reticence of Teiresias and his desire to say nothing about necessity, the energetic action of Oedipus would not have come about. And so on, and so forth. We recognize and understand Oedipus because of his reciprocal relation with Teiresias, and Teiresias becomes the figure he is because of his active relation to Oedipus. They exhibit one another and enable one another to enact that which they are. Accordingly, their relation is not a conflict but tension, discussion and juxtaposition, though not clash or collision. Conflict would have reduced their multidimensional and exceedingly complex relation to one dimension and one relation, which we might express with the formula 'he doesn't want what I want'. Therefore it is not only a matter of conflict excluding what the correlates have in common from the tense relation, but also a matter of conflict reducing the multi-layered network of differences between the correlates to a single dimension and a single level. My body or the maple under my window do not conflict with other forms of life or with the minerals in the ground, but instead are in a tense relation with all life and with the world, that is, with their particular not-I, and in a tense relation that lasts as long as life: as long as mine and that of the maple under my window. Sophocles emphasizes this superbly by allowing Oedipus' conversation with Creon, his brother-in-law, basically an apparent agon, to get much closer to a conflict than the exemplary agon of Oedipus and Teiresias. Oedipus and Creon can come into conflict because they do not have enough things in common for the differences between them to be significant and to reach the requisite degree of validity, but the relation between Oedipus and Teiresias is tension and has to remain tense, for it is a relation that lasts as long as the life of the correlates in question.

III   Not tension but conflict

At this point I should note something that occurred to me when I remembered that my body and the maple both participate in life's endless ocean. The idea gained ground in dramaturgy that the basis of drama was not tension but conflict at roughly the same time when the philosophic notion became popular that humans should, must and could 'subdue nature'. Furthermore, they could 'subdue nature' only if they were in conflict with it and with other forms of life, but that would be possible only if we withdrew from the mighty flow of life. Fortunately, we did not do this, for we are still alive (and I hope we cannot do this), and we have merely accepted the mathematical approach as a model, indeed almost as the sole relevant way of thinking that offers us secure knowledge and produces unequivocal conditions. Nevertheless, this way of thinking does not possess the necessary tools for apprehending body and life, with the probable result that we simply cease to apprehend and enquire about the body, life and other highly-complex phenomena. I think that is the only reason why we imagined that we had 'subdued nature', and that that is the only reason why we might believe that the basis of drama is conflict, although we are well-acquainted with excellent dramas without conflict, whereas we certainly cannot recall a single good one that is free from tension. Univocality and 'subduing nature' largely mean the end of life, just as conflict usually brings a drama to a close. Drama lasts as long as it is based on tension, but as soon as conflict breaks out, it veers to a close. Another fact supports this. Dramatic tension is the relation of two subjects, whereas modern mathematical thought says that only one subject is possible: the thinker.

The notion of subject introduces a level into the discussion that shows that the question of the identity of a living creature becomes even more complex than was supposed hitherto, if this being is endowed with or doomed as a result of mind. Mind opens up the being to time, language and the beyond. Am I just and exclusively the subject composing these lines? Certainly not, since this I is vastly different from the I that complains to a friend about sleeplessness, and from the I that tells a beautiful woman how much she is admired, and from the I that creates the characters in my novels, and from the I that talks to my wife. And then my I that teaches the students of comparative literature in Sarajevo is utterly different from my I that taught students of European literature in Berlin. Is my identity, and am I no more than what I am currently thinking, feeling, believing and doing, or am I everything that I ever have been, and have thought, felt, believed and done? Where, if not in me, is that I that harked back to a garden glimpsed some 30 years ago in Mostar, and that I that wanted to be an olive tree because it would have been good to be one? And if it is in me, how does that I relate to this one now that takes such trouble to be rational, disciplined and precise?

IV Language and complexity

Language opens us up to others, and I can have a language for my own use only if I share it with others. Openness to others in language means that my interlocutor is always immanently present in my utterance. Even when I merely spread knowledge about 'poetological' problems, the people whom I am addressing are present in my discourse, and if not in my choice of vocabulary, then certainly in the rhythm, tonality, syntax and modalities of what I say. You don't speak in exactly the same way to a group and to a single person; you don't address two or three in precisely that way; you don't say it in the same way to a young and to a mature audience, a woman and a man, a colleague and someone whose job you have no idea of, a close friend and someone you scarcely know: in all these cases you will never speak in exactly the same way, even about the weather and football. However little we are aware of the fact, the person we are talking to is immanently present in the way in which we talk, and even if not in what we say then always in the way in which we speak, because the person we are addressing is one of the boundaries of our essential nature in language. In consideration of the fact that humans are linguistic beings, the others, those to whom we speak, seem to comprise one of the boundaries of our identity: that is, one of the parameters over against which our identity is constantly renewed.

Of course, that does not mean that those who speak to others (and we are always talking to other people) are non-existent or entities without form or substance, but merely that the boundary of human identity is produced and shaped in a tense relation to those addressed. Heraclitus, one of the few thinkers who has made an effort to conceive of the process in question, said that you could not enter the same stream twice, because the water would always be different. That is certainly true, but it is equally true that the river which I enter between Konjic and Mostar is always the Neretva, irrespective of the fact that the water is constantly changing. I think that this image is a good illustration of the nature of human identity and how it operates. The boundary is continually rebuilt in the relation of tension to the addressee or to the actual object of the subject's action, but it is always a person. That is roughly the case with humans as linguistic beings. It is impossible to conceive of human identity proficiently if you do not take the other dimensions of mental and spiritual human nature into account, since human are just as much creatures of time and of transcendence. Are people really what they were at one particular time in their lives? I am afraid so, for that is a wholly plausible explanation of the confused and perplexing inconsistency (of people) with themselves, which surely sets them apart from dead things. (I do not know whether that sets us apart from plants and animals, since I do not know whether the maple remembers the leaves of yesteryear and the branches it has lost, and whether it feels the absence of the buds that never developed properly because a branch was snapped off). Our transcendental dimension has ordained our possession of an outer and an inner aspect, or even an outer and an inner nature, so that the two aspects are never equal and can never be reduced one to the other. Information and facts can neither describe nor delineate, let alone express, the human identity, because they are evidence only of external observation of a human being. Various authorities certainly have more information about me than my wife, yet she certainly knows me better than all those authorities taken together.

Cultural identities as well as cultures and individual cultural phenomena are similarly complex (Goethe and Oswald Spengler have shown more than convincingly that cultures are organic phenomena, if not by their nature, then at any rate by their degree of complexity, which is like that of a living creature). Consequently, any form of consideration seeking to understand cultural identities and their interactions has to adapt its methods and tools to the nature of these identities. We shall have experienced nothing about a work of art, a novel for instance, when we have collected all the facts associated with it, beginning with the author's name and his origin, continuing with the number of pages and the price, and concluding with the number of copies sold and the prizes awarded. Information and facts, every external observation and everything that might be learnt by viewing it from without, will not have got us any closer to the work of art. It is much the same with the system of ritual practices associated with the table in a certain culture, with the ceremonies of any religion, or, we might say, with the marriage rites of a culture: in such cases of external observation, however precise and original the observation, nothing will be revealed and nothing explained. Only the experience 'of the outward nature' (of the body) will empower the understanding and knowledge of the inward nature, and both together will afford knowledge of the whole. This is also the case of the relations between individual cultural phenomena and cultures. They can come into conflict only if they undergo a process of radical simplification, and if violence is done to their nature. Don Quixote may be described as a parody of the chivalric romances but is not in conflict with them; naturalist literature deviates radically from romantic literature but is not and cannot be in conflict with it, since these two literary paradigms mutually display and reciprocally form a complex and fruitfully tense relationship. They could be said to be in conflict only if they were so simplified that the entire, infinitely many-layered complex of 'naturalist literature' was quite violently reduced to the straightforward designation 'non-romantic', and the whole complex of 'romantic literature' was reduced to the ridiculous designation 'non-naturalist'.

What I have already stressed as true of the individual identity of a human being applies to the identity of a culture and a cultural phenomenon. It is as ever-changing as a river, yet remains constant. Individual works illuminate and enhance one another, enter into a reciprocal dialogue, and interrogate each other (it is important to remind ourselves continually of Mikhail Bakhtin's inspiring vision of the 'universe of meaning' where literary works dwell outside time and space and communicate with each other), constantly changing their aspect depending on their particular 'interlocutor', yet always persisting as the specific work that each and every one is. Goethe's *Faust* has one aspect when it comes into contact with Bulgakov's *Master and Margarita*, and a quite different one when it touches on Rutebeuf's miracle play *The Miracle of Theophil*. But in each case it remains Goethe's *Faust*.

If we avoid the simplifications of univocal rationalism and insist that relations between cultural identities are dependent not on conflict but on tension, that does not mean that we call in question the existence of individual identities and the possibility of distinguishing between them. We only assert that 'I' cannot be reduced to 'not you', just as Christianity cannot be reduced to 'not Buddhism', because 'I' and Christianity would sacrifice their authentic identity if violently reduced in any such way. Those who maintain that as long as Islam and Christianity remain true to themselves they will not and cannot come into conflict, do not assert that they cannot be distinguished from one another, but merely acknowledge the nature of religion. If they go on to say that the boundaries between Islam and Christianity are not unambiguous and are not always well-defined, and that the relations between these two religions are not one-dimensional and on one level, and if they say that these religions have a lot in common, and find the common features significant, and the differences valid, I am quite certain that the foregoing is entirely true. The proponents of this view will not have said, and will not say, that the two religions cannot be distinguished one from the other, and that they surrender 'their identities in the ecumenical rhetoric of love which do-gooders force us to adopt'. On the contrary, by referring to common characteristics, I have helped people to perceive and value the differences that are so considerable that these two religions certainly could not be resolved into a 'syncretistic religion', as some fear would be the case.

V   Difference and differences

For instance, we have the difference in the nature of the ontological distinction. In Islam the difference between the Creator and the creature cannot be bridged, but can merely be 'broken through', cancelled, erased for a moment, by the Creator, by revelation for instance. But that too happens only by the power of the word, which means by the word as a reflection of the Divine. The revelation (of the Qur'an) is a translation of God's message, and the angel Gabriel translated the revelation into a language accessible to human beings, so that the Messenger of Islam, Mohammed, could receive and understand it. The difference in Christianity is that Christianity promises that the ontological difference between Creator and creation can be bridged. If I have understood the matter correctly, human beings can even overcome the difference by believing in and following Jesus, who has already bridged the gap. Expressed in a simplified form, we may say that the basis of Christianity is provided by the God made human, or human made God, who has bridged the ontological difference and has thereby given every human being the opportunity, or at least the hope, that he or she will be able to do the same. But the Mother of the book (*umm-ul-kitab*, the non-verbal ur-version of all sacred books and of the Holy Qur'an) is the basis of Islam. The individual revelations (the Zend Avesta, the Old Testament, the New Testament, the Qur'an) are reflections, parts or impressions of the Mother of the book translated into human languages. How is this book written? Using ideas, or significations pure and simple, or in a virtual or self-contained language? We do not know, cannot know, for we can obtain access to its reflections only in a translation prepared by an angel (in the case of the Qur'an it was the angel Gabriel). Beyond the Mother of the book there is God, of whom we cannot even say that he exists, since he is the author of existence. He is the source of all existence and may not even be placed among existents.

This difference, which is only one in a series of fruitful and immeasurably important differences between the two religions, is apparent in every area of life and thought, in everyday human actions, and in poetry, philosophy and the rites of both religions. Even in mysticism, which of its nature calls boundaries in question, it can be neither neglected nor ignored, and is more than merely evident. Rabbiyya al-Adawiyya and Teresa of Avila celebrated love mystical and absolute, although there is no mention of the 'sacred bridegroom' in Rabiyya, which would be blasphemous in that culture. Differences of that kind between the two religions occur at every step and turn in texts and in everyday rites, and in thought and feeling, but they are significant only for those who are also aware of what they have in common, and rejoice at differences and similarities.

Translated by J. G. Cumming

Narration and Identity

ALEKSANDAR HEMON

If identity is essentially constituted by narration, by stories that every individual can freely develop, democracy means a space where storytelling is made possible, where stories of individuals can meet to mingle with other stories. Therefore ethnic storytelling is undemocratic. Balkan countries need to learn good storytelling.

I'm not an expert on identity or narration, let alone theology. But I'm legally identified as Aleksandar Hemon, and I'm (much like the rest of humanity) a thinking storyteller. And I'm also someone who writes and operates simultaneously in two languages and cultures. So I do have a few things to say about narration and identity.

First, let me tell you a true story: Four years ago, my nine-month-old daughter Isabel was diagnosed with an aggressively malignant brain tumour. She subsequently underwent eight operations and several cycles of chemotherapy, none of which helped. 108 days after her diagnosis, she died.

It was a horrendous time for my wife and me, as it was difficult for our daughter Ella, Isabel's older sister, who was nearly three at the time. It's hard to know whether Isabel's diagnosis and suffering triggered it, but at the beginning of our family ascent to Golgotha (at the end of which there was not an inkling of salvation), Ella came up with an imaginary sibling, who soon acquired the name Mingus (after Charlie Mingus, the great jazz musician) and was initially embodied in a blue inflatable doll of a space alien.

Ella would tell us tales of Mingus, their complicated plots not quite coherent nor comprehensible, partly because they never had a proper beginning or ending. Now and then, we'd witness Ella's playing with Mingus – the alien or the fully imaginary one – administering fictional medicine or taking his temperature, using the vocabulary she had collected

73

on her visits to the hospital, or from our talking about Isabel's illness. She'd tell us that Mingus had a tumour, was undergoing tests, but was going to get better in two weeks. Once Mingus even had a little sister named Isabel – entirely distinct from Ella's sister – who also had a tumour and was also going to get better in two weeks. Whatever accidental knowledge of Isabel's illness Ella was accumulating, whatever words she was picking up from participating in our experience, she was processing through her imaginary brother. To her Mingus was a means to comprehend what was going on. She was missing her sister, so Mingus gave her some comfort in that respect as well, even if at some point he shed his inflatable earthly body to become exclusively imaginary, yet no less real for that.

After Isabel died, Mingus lived on. His age ranged between three and 25, and he acquired and lost various abilities. He stayed with us a lot, but he also lived around the corner with his parents and a variable number of siblings, most often including two brothers, Jackon and Cliff, and a sister, Piccadilly. One day, Ella was suspiciously quiet in her room, and I asked her what she'd been doing. She told me she'd been watching movies made by Mingus's mother. Ella didn't have a TV or computer in her room – the movies were projected on the screen of her imagination.

Occasionally, Mingus had his own children – three sons, at one point. When we went skiing, Mingus preferred snowboarding. When we went to London for Christmas, Mingus went to Nebraska. Sometimes he yelled at Ella ('Shut up, Mingus!', she'd yell back); other times he'd lose his own voice, but then he'd speak in Isabel's. At some point, he was a magician. With his magic wand, Ella was hoping, he would make Isabel reappear.

Once, early in Mingus's life, I asked Ella what Mingus was doing at that exact moment. He was throwing a tantrum in the other room, she said. Another time, a couple of year later, I asked Ella how it was possible that she always talked about Mingus but I never got to see him. She said: 'Tata, he's imaginary!', and chuckled, as though finding it hard to believe I wasn't aware of that simple and obvious fact.

I realized that, for Ella, there was no conflict between the real and the imaginary. Not only were they not mutually exclusive, they were in fact mutually reinforcing – the real had to be imagined to be real; the imaginary was fully realized only when it became real. It might not surprise you if I claim that the collusion of the imaginary and the real is essential to our life as adults as well. Consider memory or, for that matter, faith: by necessity they contain the real and the imaginary at the same time, and they're indistinguishable.

Earlier this year, Ella announced that she was done with Mingus and his existence. My wife and I were truly sad that he was so abruptly retired – we had got used to him, and we missed him. What ultimately made his existence superficial was Ella's reading ability (in French and English). She no longer had to generate imaginary characters and narratives, because they were now available to her in all the books she was reading.

The life of Mingus (which lasted some three and a half years) coincided with the phase in Ella's development marked with rapid language acquisition and cognitive advancement – the period when she suddenly had a lot of language and information that needed processing. The stories of Mingus were the processing, the result of which was knowledge. The narratization of her experience – both the imaginary and the real aspects of it – was essential for her developing what might be considered reflective consciousness, a sense of having a self distinct from others, Mingus's included, a self capable of reflecting upon its position in time and in the world, upon its presence among other people and its relation to them. By telling stories of Mingus, Ella was becoming herself. She assembled her identity by way of narration, by learning how to tell stories.

The kind of work that Ella has done is what we have all done at some point in our lives to end up with a sense of possessing a unique consciousness – a sense of having an identity. If Walter R. Fisher is right in claiming that 'the world as we know it is a set of stories that must be chosen among in order for us to live life in a process of continual re-creation'.[1] then Ella was figuring out how to identify, create and reproduce those stories under the conditions that differentiated her consciousness from others.

One of the features of consciousness is what might be called (after Julian Jaynes) the Analogue I, the projected self, different from the self we wake up with. For example: after my few weeks in Sarajevo, I'm going to Barcelona, where I've never been. But I've already imagined myself (as I perceive myself presently) in Barcelona, which I've also imagined – in other words, I deploy my Analogue I to Barcelona in the exactly same way as Ella deployed Mingus. So that when I arrive in Catalonia, there will have to be a reconciliation – or, rather, a merger – between the real and the imaginary Barcelona, as well as between me and my Analogue I. In these reconciliations my identity is actualized: I am not only what I am, but also what I would and could be. I become who I am by identifying my possibilities. I am I + my Analogue I. I am my own Mingus.

Similarly, we can talk about an Analogue I that follows a path parallel to the path of my bodily self – parallel in the sense of 'two lines meeting in infinity'. Thus I'm often asked if I ever imagine what my life would have been like if I'd stayed in Sarajevo for the siege. I seldom imagine my entire life under siege – knowing that I could have been killed the first day – but I've imagined myself in the moments, some of them requiring difficult ethical and moral choices, I never could have actually lived through, as I was in Chicago for the entirety of the siege. But to know who I am, I have to imagine what I could be and/or could have been. It's hard for me to conceive of a moral person who does not imagine alternative moral choices in his or her striving to pick the right one. We test our morality in the laboratory of imagination; Mingus and the Analogue I are commonly deployed for moral purposes. For example: I've asked myself what I would have done if I'd had a choice between running under sniper fire to drag a wounded person into safety or staying safe under cover? Because I imagine myself as a decent person, I prefer to think I'd have chosen to save a fellow human being. Even if, honestly, I don't and can't know, I've still tested both possibilities in my imagination. We establish our moral identity not only by accumulating moral decisions in our 'real' life, but by imagining narrative situations in which such decisions would be made.

Barring serious mental problems, we wake up every morning believing that at our core is the same self as yesterday, expecting it to be the same tomorrow, just as we can gather all the disparate sensations, thoughts and emotions – happening all the time and simultaneously – under the flag of the same unique self. We are the main characters in the complicated, confusing stories of our lives, which we learned how to tell – to ourselves and to others – at Ella's age. We wake up knowing the story of our identity – how we became who we are – and we expect it to continue.

Which is to say that another important requirement for establishing our identity is diachronic and synchronic sequencing of our life. To comprehend and maintain ourselves as a unique entity, we narratively connect our past, our present and our future: the story of my life has the same main character whether he's four, 40 or 80 years old – that is my synchronic self, simultaneously present in the past, present and future. At the same time, everything that is happening to me now can be put in the narrative sequence of my life, the trajectory along which my self has progressed (or regressed) for the last 50 years. Even if I couldn't undertake that operation at this exact instant, I can already anticipate the way this endless moment, this multitudinous day, fits into the narrative of who I am. I contain my own multitudes and I can narrate them.

We live inside a narrative space that starts out as sovereign – as our own – and always strives to be so. But the story is never just my own, as our sovereign spaces overlap: in the family, in the society, in common human experience. No one is the exclusive narrator of their own story, nor can it be knowable without the presence and interference of others. This is why we are biologically, evolutionarily compelled to tell each other about our lives – storytelling is not just a form of expression, nor is it merely communication, it's a means of acquiring, sharing and organizing human knowledge. Our stories are unknowable and/or meaningless without all the other stories. As Fisher suggests, following Kenneth Burke: 'One's life is … a story that participates in the stories of those who have lived, who live now, and who will live in the future.'[2]

The narrative models for establishing that sovereign space – its borders, as it were – come from the outside, with language acquisition and attendant socialization. Ella's early narratives of Mingus thus had no head nor tail, no beginning, middle nor end, neither conclusion nor closure, no gradual development – she didn't know that stories could or should have those things. Quickly, however, the Mingus narratives began to assume their shapes based on stories she was receiving from us, from books and movies. Once she asked me (far too early, as she was about five) how babies were made. I avoided anatomical details and focused on the narrative of love – Mommy and Tata met, fell in love, made love and so on. She kept insisting, and I told her some more, but still not answering all the questions she wanted answered. She fell silent for a minute and then retold me what I'd just told her as a story of Mingus (who was 25) who met his girlfriend, fell in love with and moved in with her and so forth. I provided her with a narrative template, and she instantly applied it.

For millennia, from Gilgamesh until this very moment, literature has provided narrative models for understanding our position and situation in the universe. Hayden White suggests that 'narrative is a metacode, a human universal on the basis of which trans-cultural messages about the shared reality can be transmitted … the absence of narrative capacity or a refusal of narrative indicates an absence or refusal of meaning itself'.[3] We can understand Gilgamesh as we can Madame Bovary, despite all the markers of particular societies and belief systems they came from, because we are conditioned to understand and identify with stories about people – and all stories are always about people. Fisher again: 'Narratives enable us to understand the actions of others because we all live out narratives in our lives and because we understand our own lives in terms of narratives.[4]

By the way, Flaubert's Emma Bovary provides a great example of (mis)adoption of external narrative models. She reconceived the narrative of herself based on the model coming from sentimental novels, which tragically collided with the rigid model of provincial bourgeois life.

The moral, ethical and political question related to the narration of sovereign identity is this: who gets to provide the structure for the story of my life? Or, the same question put differently: who gets do decide who I really am? Or: who determines my identity?

One way to understand bigotry, discrimination and racism is to see them as violations of individual narrative sovereignty by the imposition of reductive external models: people are diminished to narratives they have no agency in, and their human potential is limited by delimiting their narrative space and defining their identity. So that women, for example, are reduced to serving men, non-heterosexuals are reduced to the closet, people of colour are reduced to the domain of submission and violence, and people of different ethnicities are shrunk to congenital mutual animosity and genetically conditioned hatred.

An essential aspect of individual sovereignty is the right and ability to speak for oneself in unrestricted public space and participate in the political process without fear for one's private domain. Because narrative agency is directly related to the possession of language – both are acquired at the same time – storytelling is inherently democratic, as anyone, barring mental disability, can partake in it. This is why freedom of speech is essential to any serious attempt at democracy, as is respect for one's private space. In any decent democracy everyone's right to tell and live out their story is inviolable and, indeed, sacred.

Which is why the state of Bosnia and Herzegovina is constitutionally and undemocratically set up to violate individual sovereignty.

As we all well know, the carriers of sovereignty in Bosnia are the three constitutive peoples, who need not be named. In other words, the only stories that really matter are the stories of those three ethnicities – everyone in between, like Ambassador Finci or Mr. Sejdic or, for that matter, me –

are reduced to irrelevant oddities who have no narrative representation in the public space.

The dominant collective narratives in this country are ready-made and recycled, very poorly imagined, featuring a small cast of greatly repulsive characters. They only know the plots in which nations are the ones with agency, while the narrative arcs of national suppression, suffering and redemption subsume all individual stories. In those dominant narratives, identities are not chosen but are given at birth, only to be reinforced through ethnic education (which edits out all the stories that might contradict the dominant models) and confirmed by an exclusionary, segregated political system that takes collective identity to be axiomatically self-evident.

Ethnic storytelling bothers me as an ethical person who believes in individual narrative sovereignty, as a citizen who craves justice and equality. But it also bothers me as a professional, committed storyteller. Everyone knows that all good stories end up being true, because they are related to our deepest human identity. The narrators of Bosnia and Herzegovina as it is now are lazy bastards, incapable of saying anything without telling a lie. It's a high time for some true and good stories, for some richer, more productive identities, for some positive characters.

Notes

1. Walter R. Fisher, *Human Communication as Narration: Toward a Philosophy of Reason, Value and Action*, Columbia, 1987, p. 65.
2. *Ibid.*, p. 63.
3. *Ibid.*, p. 65.
4. *Ibid.*, p. 66.

Part Three: The Religious Potential for Peace

Religious and Political Identities in Bosnia and Herzegovina

DINO ABAZOVIĆ

In this article I examine problematical aspects of the present transitional phase in Bosnia and Herzegovina, with an emphasis on religious revival and the specific nexus of ethnic and political interpretations of the historic part played by religion in forming the dominant ethnic groups in the country. Some attention is also given to the phenomenon of religious nationalism in Bosnia and Herzegovina.

I Introduction

In any description or discussion of the West Balkans, it is essential not to forget the following: 'It has never been possible to confirm with any degree of accuracy the extent to which faith is a question of individual experience, and a matter of experiences of spiritual need in relation to the sacred, God or transcendence. It has also proved impossible to decide when it became open to use by a collectivist form of identification, always with a fully active and close relation to politics and ideology, while remaining vulnerable to manipulation and instrumentalization, sometimes with the most disastrous results.'[1]

In fact, it is a commonplace of historical circumstances that religion of all things is the absolutely indisputable *differentia specifica*, or characteristic aspect, of the collective identities of the resident population, and that denominational identities have proved to be the decisive factor in the development of the ethnic-national/collective identities that are still dominant today in Bosnia and Herzegovina. How much influence and what significance in context are still to be ascribed to religion in society remains debatable. From a sociological viewpoint, however, the emphasis is on the influence of an organized religion, or of actual religious communities, on

83

other autonomous and semi-autonomous spheres of social life in Bosnia and Herzegovina. However that may be, over the last two decades we have certainly observed religion becoming an incontrovertible political fact in Bosnia and Herzegovina, and a change in the position of organized religion.

Compared with the previous phase of a basic order of social relations dominated by a situation of 'theisms without any function', from now on we also have a 'theism with exceptionally important public functions'.[2] If we exclude Bosnia and Herzegovina for the moment, the start of the new century has been characterized by a universally notable process of religious reawakening or awakening of religious sentiments, which has occurred in the very environment from which it seemed absent at a certain stage: that is, in the 'West'.

II   Religion and nationalism

At this point, it is necessary to recall certain essential theoretical approaches to the interpretation of religion and nationalism that will help readers to understand my own thinking on the present topic.

As Peter Van Der Veer and Hartmuth Lehman remark in their introduction to the symposium *Nation and Religion: Perspectives on Europe and Asia*,[3] ('Western') social theory often made a preliminary a priori ideological distinction between the nationalist and the religious imagination. In the past, such arguments maintained that nationalism formed part of justifiable modern political reality. It was taken for granted that nationalism was 'secular', all the more so since it was assumed to evolve as part of the process of secularization and modernization. As far as these and similar views are concerned, religion is politically relevant only in countries in the underdeveloped world, which was also the case in the Western world at a certain time in the past. If, however, religion appears in a political context in the modern world, it is called 'fundamentalism'.

Therefore it is important to note, according to Van Der Veer and Lehmann, that the 'nation' and 'religion' have entered relevant theory as universal categories of Western modernity, and that their universality is located mainly in the history of Western expansionism.[4]

Even though in the past theoretical approaches to relations between the modern nation and the modern State (with a few exceptions) ignored the influence and role of religion, attitudes have changed in recent years. Accordingly, the symposium in question emphasizes the fact that nationalism does indeed determine the future and redemption of humanity to a considerable degree. But this would seem to dispense with an essential aspect of the real aims of redemption or conquest of the future. We also have to ask if it is appropriate (as the symposium would seem to imply) to interpret nationalism not as a substitute religion but as an authentic form of religion.

III Secularization and fixation on religion

One way to understand why any such approach to this question was formulated is to acknowledge the results of early secularization even at the time when the first European national States were founded. This process should be seen as a secularization of concepts of the (Judaeo-Christian) tradition of belief, or as its 'translation' into a vernacular form. The relevant literature refers most often to concepts such as the Chosen People, the Promised Land, messianism and fraternity (fraternity in the sense of *communio sanctorum* [communion of saints]) as notions that operated subsequently in accordance with the new understanding of a proto-national group. Moreover, in the same historical perspective, the attendant implementation and extension of religious freedom was considered to be a possible method of conflict avoidance, while any restriction of religious freedom was viewed as a source of conflict. But here too we are faced with a characteristic paradox: perhaps 'religions' were used more in order to provoke conflicts, rather than as means of resolving them. One thing is almost certain: from an historical viewpoint, the freedom to exercise religion and religious freedom is an exception and never the rule.

However that may be, religions played a central role in the shaping of many European national identities (and this was the case not only in former Yugoslavia but in Poland, Ireland, Britain and Greece), and we are now experiencing an updating of Carl Schmitt's argument about a common structure of theological and political concepts.[5] The process accords with Schmitt's assertion that: 'All important concepts of modern state theory are secularized theological concepts. Not only because of their historical development at a time when they were transferred from theology to the theory of the State, where for instance almighty God become the omnipotent lawgiver, but also because of their systematic structure, an avowal that is necessary for a sociological understanding of these concepts. An exception in jurisprudence is equivalent to a miracle in theology. An awareness of these equivalences is absolutely necessary to decide exactly how philosophical ideas evolved by way of the State in past centuries.'[6]

In fact, Schmitt's arguments especially were also addressed in the most recent debates about religion in public discussion, especially in the dialogue between Charles Taylor and Jürgen Habermas.[7] In the present respect, however, it seems more apposite to consider Taylor's call for a 'radical redefinition of secularism' and his objection to Habermas's 'fixation on religion', a position which in Taylor's opinion Habermas shares with John Rawls and others. According to Taylor, there is no reason to identify the position of religion in public opinion as a 'special case', although he concedes that this had long been the case as the result of a whole series of historical suasions. In his view, there is no reason to treat religion separately from other, non-religious world-views when seeking to define the question of state neutrality.

IV   Liberal public opinion

There is certainly no doubt of the relevance here of Habermas's entirely cogent insistence that we should focus mainly on public opinion in modern liberal societies. Nevertheless, it is also important to take into account those critics who remind us that the very same liberal societies exclude people who are different, as well as certain types of claim, from serious consideration. From the earliest days, in fact, liberal public opinion excluded such categories as women, the impecunious or religious minorities.

Therefore I think that Talal Asad is right to assert with regard to this kind of criticism of liberal democracy that public opinion not merely offers no more than a forum for rational debate, but an area of exclusion. Of course, we should not forget that (liberal) public opinion is an area that is unavoidably (not only unpredictably) articulated from a power basis. For this very reason 'an organized religion will often demand a public role, and attribute its necessity to the fact that society has taken the wrong path, and needs an injection of religious values to return to the strait and narrow way. Religion will try to "deprivatize" itself so that it is entitled to a voice in current debates about social and poilitical tendencies. The aim is to become a major factor in political deliberalization, and to make sure that the voice of religion is taken into consideration.'[8]

In Bosnia and Herzegovina, however, in contradistinction to the period when we were subject to the previous basic form of socio-political order of a Socialist mould (in Tito's Yugoslavia), when the customary situation featured the abovementioned theisms without any public role, we are now witnessing the establishment of what is essentially a more ethnic–political system, and to the enjoyment of an unusually important public role by the said theisms. It is a quite different question how far the representatives of organized religion were, and still are, prepared to meet the expectations facing them.

V   Religion, politics and symbols

I have argued elsewhere[9] that it is most important for politics and its relations with religion, just as Genevieve Zubrzycki showed with regard to Poland,[10] that political institutions and symbols should not be sacralized here and become the objects of religious adulation. Instead, the tendency has been rather for religious symbols to be secularized and re-sacralized as national symbols. That gives ethnic–national politics the opportunity to mobilize a great number of followers by using religious arguments which, however, are advanced primarily to achieve extra-religious ends.

The opening up of religion in the direction of public opinion is also qualified as deprivatization, and this process has proved decisive from the 1980s to the present day. Even Steve Bruce,[11] who is among the last 'defenders of the secularization thesis', also recognizes occasions when modernity does not undermine religion but may allocate important social roles to religion. Such cases concern situations of cultural defence and cultural change.

Cultural defence occurs when two or more communities come into conflict and their members are heirs to different religious traditions (Protestants and Catholics in Northern Ireland; Serbs, Croats and Bosniaks in former Yugoslavia). Then the social significance of religious identity may become more important, and evoke a call for ethnic unity and pride. The situation is similar when one community dominates another (with another religion or 'none'), so that in such cases the religious institution assumes the role of defender of the culture and identity of the dominated citizens. In situations of cultural change, religious institutions come to play a supportive role on behalf of people, in order to come to terms with the changes they have to face.

In fact, religious communities (and religion) were the main sources of resistance to the former Socialist regime, and influenced almost all social structures (institutional and cognitive). In this sense, nothing else had anything like so great and effective a power, so that in addition to all other outcomes it also constituted an area of reference for the preservation and transmission of national cultures and their concomitant values.

At the same time (as Mark Juergensmeyer observed), on a global stage that saw the 'downfall of national States and the disillusionment of old forms of secular nationalism, we experienced the opening up of both the opportunity for new nationalisms and the need for them ... In the modern political climate, religious and ethnic nationalisms duly offered solutions to repair the supposed inadequacies of Western-style secular politics. Since secular references began to grow weaker in the post-Soviet and post-colonial era, local leaders began to search for new berths for their social identities and political loyalties.'[12]

VI   Religious nationalism and ethnicization

In the Western Balkans, all the abovementioned tendencies came to a head in a form of religious nationalism. This particular nationalism 'evolved from modern institutional heterologies ... and extended the institutional logic of religion in the area of a democratic national State, by deriving its authority from God's absolute commandment, and not by the subjective generation of the people themselves'.[13]

Religious nationalism is a special form of collective presentation and a new ontology of power. Since religion is selected as the exclusive basis of the national collective identity, this is a form of politicized religion and 'religionized' politics (in which politics is conceived of as a religious duty). The aim pursued is a re-ordering of social relations on the basis of pseudo-religious elements and functions.

Religious nationalists in Bosnia and Herzegovina think of the relationship between nation and denomination almost in the sense that any change in the national identity (which is taken as equivalent to the denominational identity) is interpreted as a humiliation for the nation. But no account is taken here of the fact that by their very nature the dominant religions to which the population of Bosnia and Herzegovina belong are universal, and therefore not particular. But religious nationalists are particular: that is, their doctrine is a matter of a quite definite, actual community, and it relates only to those who possess not only the religious but other common characteristics of that identity – which means above all the same ethnic origin (Bosniaks, Serbs, Croats). We might say that religious nationalism in Bosnia and Herzegovina is actually one of the most up-to-date responses to modern secular individualism in the modern nation State.

At the same time, the representatives of religious nationalism oppose modern (secular) nationalism and national movements, whose theoretical and ideological principles insist on a dominance of the (supra)national over and above other identities and affiliations (such as those of a denominational or historical nature). Therefore, religious nationalism is positively related to its predecessors that opposed the creation of a common state identity: that is, of an identity achieved by assimilation as inclusion and involvement as citizens of civil society.

Furthermore, it is 'of central importance that ethnicization once again establishes the precedence of the political over all other spheres, so that solutions are looked for in the political realm, whether that is appropriate at this point or not. From this moment on, an attempt is made to determine political programmes in accordance with the ethnic and ethnicized nation rather than in line with the civil identity, so that ideas, goals and future are mobilized and interpreted in conformity with the imperatives of ethnicity ... This means that societies almost lose the capability of defining their goals on the basis of material civil criteria, and of communicating in any other way than by talking about ethnicity and a personal loyalty.'[14] And in Bosnia and Herzegovina, ethnicity is constructed definitively (everything else may be a matter for dispute, but not this) on the basis of one's denomination.

Finally, to ensure that a functionality of multiethnic and multidenominational societies is achieved in the political field, one of the first interventions must involve a necessary reinstitutionalization of the public realm, but only after an essential demystification of ethnic and denominational (ir)rationalities, especially when they result from religious nationalisms.

Translated by John Maxwell

Dino Abazović

Notes

1. Ivan Lovrenović, 'Pitanje iz života, pitanje iz vjere', in Thomas Bremer (ed.), *Religija, društvo,politika: kontroverzna tumačenjap*, Bonn, 2002, p. 330.
2. Srđan Vrcan, *Vjera u vrtlozima tranzicije, Dalmatinska akcija*, Split, 2001.
3. Peter Van Der Veer & Hartmuth Lehman (eds), *Nation and Religion: Perspectives on Europe and Asia*, Princeton, NJ, 1999, pp. 1–4 (In this article, quotations from English-language publications have been back-translated from Bosnian or Serbo-Croat versions).
4. *Ibid.*, p. 5.
5. Carl Schmitt, *Political Theology*, Cambridge, MA, 1985.
6. *Cf.* Talal Asad, 'Religion, Nation-State, Secularism', in Peter Van Der Veer & Hartmuth Lehman (eds), *Nation and Religion: Perspectives on Europe and Asia, op. cit.*, p. 184.
7. C. Calhoun, E. Mendieta & J. Van Antwepern (eds), *The Power of Religion in Public Space*, New York, 2012.
8. Jeff Haynes, *Religion in Global Politics*, London & New York, 1998, p. 19.
9. Dino Abazović, 'Religija u svojim vezama sa politikom', *Dijalog* 3–4, Sarajevo, 2014.
10. Genevieve Zubrzycki, *The Crosses of Auschwitz: Nationalism and Religion in Post-Communist Poland*, Chicago, 2006.
11. Steve Bruce, *Religion in the Modern World: From Cathedrals to Cult*, Oxford & New York, 1996.
12. Mark Juergensmayer, 'Religious Terror and Secular State', Study Paper, Global and Intl. Study Program, Washington D.C, 2004, p. 5.
13. Roger Friedland, 'Religious Nationalism and the Problem of Collective Representation', *Annual Review of Sociology* 27 (2001), p. 142.
14. George Schöpflin, 'Civilno društvo i nacionalitet', in Vukašin Pavlović (ed.), *Potisnuto civilno društvo*, Eko centar, Belgrade, 1995, p. 164.

Liberation Hermeneutics through the I's/Eyes of the (Female) Moor

SAROJINI NADAR

The objective of this article is to explore the extent to which the Bible holds possibilities for peace in a post-conflict society. I grapple with the question of the role of liberation theology, or, more specifically, biblical liberation hermeneutics, in post-apartheid South Africa, and suggest that some theoretical and paradigm shifts in liberation hermeneutics are needed if holistic liberation is ever to be realized. Using Anouar Majid's concept of 'the Moor' as a heuristic tool, I try to examine the complexity and nuances of liberation hermeneutics, particularly in post-conflict societies.

I Introduction

Reflecting on religion and identity in a post-conflict society requires some self-identification. I am a fourth-generation South African Indian Christian woman. My ancestors were brought to South Africa by the British as 'indentured labourers' – a euphemism for slaves – to work on the sugar plantations. Indians commemorated 150 years of being in South Africa in 2010. According to the mid-year population estimates of South Africa,[1] South Africa has a total population of about 50 million people. Of these, 40 million are classified as African; Whites and so-called Coloureds are about 4,5 million each; and Indians account for about 1.2 million of the population. At 2.5 per cent of the population, Indians are technically a minority in South Africa. However, the status of being an Indian minority in South Africa is not the equivalent of being an Indian minority in the USA, for example. Our minority status was complicated by apartheid, which classified us as 'non-white', which essentially grouped Indians with their African counterparts, though in varying illogical degrees. It was 'really less about number and more about power',[2] as Bailey *et al*. assert.

Notwithstanding my specific functional racial classification, ideologically, theoretically and in the daily practice of my life I consider myself to be black. I understand blackness in terms of Steve Biko's 'black consciousness', which understands black as inclusive, particularly in the South African context. Furthermore, Biko considers blackness to be more than a matter of skin pigmentation, and as a reflection of mental attitude.[3]

As a South African, you can never quite escape race as a discursive category. This is illustrated very well in the following story of my experience of moving house in 2010, and the subsequent challenges of trying to find schools for my children. While this might be thought to be a narrative 'detour', it is very much a part of the methodology of this article.[4] The primary reason we wanted to move house was to move to an area with better schools for our two sons, who were aged 13 and 7, and starting high school and grade 1 respectively in 2011. 'Better' schools were located in previously restricted white suburbs. Most of the good public schools are those that were reserved for white students in apartheid South Africa. In post-apartheid South Africa these good schools have seen an influx of 'other' students. Research has shown that this has caused the common 'exodus' effect, when white parents withdraw their children from these public schools and enroll them in private schools.[5] This exodus is often justified by complaints about the 'lowering of standards' and 'over-crowding'. While some previously white public schools in South Africa have simply given in to the increasing numbers of 'others' seeking entry to their schools, and have responded with an exodus, there are those who insist on restricting access on racial grounds, but couch that restriction in euphemistic terms, such as 'safeguarding standards'.

Unfortunately, I was seeking entry for my then six-year-old son into the latter type of school, the kind that restricts access on racial grounds but uses other terms to explain the rejection. After endless difficulties trying to secure even an appointment to see the principal, let alone my son's access to the school, I was eventually asked by the exasperated white school administrator, 'Do you not think that your son would be more "comfortable" in School X?' 'Why would my son be more comfortable in School X?', was my obvious question. 'Because that school has an after-school madrassa!', she declared. An after-school madrassa is where Muslim children learn Arabic and receive religious instruction. This white administrator had simply assumed that I was a Muslim. There could be a number of different explanations for her false assumption, one of which could be the perfectly 'logical' deduction that I must be Muslim since the closest area adjacent to this previously all-white suburb was one predominantly inhabited by Muslims.

Nevertheless, the central thesis of Anouar Majid's book *We are all Moors* offers another, possibly more plausible, explanation. 'What I want to show in this book', he says of his use of the term 'Moor', 'is not only someone who is religiously Muslim; even more importantly, he or she is also a figure that stands for anyone who is not considered to be part of the social mainstream'.

Majid does not stop at a 'face-value' analysis, but goes further to point to the supremacist reasoning undergirding the construction of the Moor identity. He states it pointedly in the preface to the book: 'Since the defeat of Islam in medieval Spain, minorities in the West have become in some ways reincarnations of the Moor, an enduring threat to Western civilization.'[6] In that moment of interaction with the white school administrator, my son and I were 'reincarnations of the Moor'. To all intents and purposes we could have been Hindus, Buddhists, African traditionalists, little elves or fairies. It did not matter, for we are all Moors. That is the powerful thesis to which Majid's book testifies. By means of a historical survey, based on the writings of philosophers, novelists, historians and even playwrights, Majid provides compelling evidence that the expulsion of the Moors from Europe in the sixteenth and seventeenth centuries was due to 'a lack of assimilation into the Christian national body'.[7] Most telling is the evidence he provides for the conflation of Moorish–Jewish identity in his chapter 'Muslim–Jews', which cements his thesis that we are all indeed Moors.

The questions which I try to address here are: 'How can Majid's central thesis 'We are all Moors' be brought to bear on the practice of biblical interpretation for liberation? What do the perspectives of the Moor, the I's/eyes of the Moor, offer for the enterprise of biblical hermeneutics methodologically and theoretically in post-apartheid South Africa?

II   Liberation Hermeneutics in (post-) apartheid South Africa

The role of the Bible in the struggle for liberation from apartheid in South Africa has been well documented. While the Bible was recognized as a tool of oppression and recognized as containing, and at times sanctioning, oppression,[8] even its ambivalent role in the liberation struggle was nevertheless central to theologies of liberation.[9] Justin Ukpong has noted: 'Liberation hermeneutics in general uses the Bible as a resource to struggle against oppression of any kind, based on the biblical witness that God does not sanction oppression but always stands on the side of the oppressed to liberate them.'[10]

Nevertheles, the relevance of liberation hermeneutics in post-apartheid South Africa is contested. The fundamental question which liberation theologians have been asking is: What is the role of liberation theology in a country which is 'post-liberation' and hailed as possessing one of the most significantly liberal human-rights-based constitutions in the world? If the primary struggle for liberation was racial and political – now that political liberation has been achieved – why is there a need for liberation hermeneutics?

Anouar Majid's thesis that 'we are all Moors' provides some clues. I shall now focus on some of the insights his thesis provides for the shaping of the contours of liberation biblical hermeneutics in post-apartheid South Africa.

III   Liberation hermeneutics through the I's/eyes of the Moor

The three key insights from Majid's thesis I wish to focus on are: Intersectionality, Identity and Identification.

(a) Intersectionality

To show how the notion of intersectionality is brought to life by the contention that 'we are all Moors' and functions in my analysis, I turn again to my experience of moving house. While buying our new home, I was concerned to know whether the house was close enough to the school to guarantee my sons' acceptance by their respective schools, and told the white house agent helping us how worried I was. 'Of course, you will get in.', she declared. 'They are only trying to prevent "the blacks" from getting in! Indians do well in maths and science. They want those kinds of students.' It would seem that not only are we all Moors, but some Moors are blacker than others. Perhaps some Moors have alternative sexual preferences? Perhaps some Moors have breasts? I would argue that recognizing the 'multidimensionality' of marginalized subjects' lived experiences[11] is crucial for the practice of liberation hermeneutics in post-apartheid South Africa. In other words, we have to understand that liberation from racial oppression is not the only liberation needed in South Africa. We need understanding as Patricia Hill Collins describes it, that 'systems of race, social class, gender, ethnicity, nation, and age form mutually constructing features of social organization'.[12]

Put simply, racism is sexism is homophobia is classism. The system of domination tries to institute varying degrees of 'otherness' as a paternalistic measure. Intersectionality, which is at the heart of Majid's thesis that 'we are all Moors', calls these classifications into question.

Within the guild of biblical studies in many parts of Africa, for example, it remains acceptable to practise liberation hermeneutics, but not to engage in feminist hermeneutics. Furthermore, even when feminist hermeneutics is accepted, it remains problematical to engage in queer hermeneutics. African feminist biblical scholars, womanist biblical scholars, Latin-American and Asian women biblical scholars have called and continue to call black and liberation theologies to account for not taking seriously the concerns of women within these discourses. The thesis that we are all Moors cements this call, which finds its home in minority biblical criticism in a search for 'partners in a common cause'.[13] While minority criticism provides racial and ethnic lenses for reading the Bible, Majid's thesis helps us to move beyond the 'racial–ethnic alliance'[14] to other ideological alliances. In post-apartheid South Africa, it is important to move beyond the racial–ethnic hermeneutic.

(b) Identity

The second I/eye that the Moor provides us with is the importance of identity within liberation hermeneutics. Of course, liberation hermeneutics finds its basis and meaning within the politics of identity in the discourses of biblical studies. But Majid warns that 'Identities of any sort are often more fictional than real'.[15] However, if liberation hermeneutics is about finding meaning in biblical texts because we are 'reading from this place', then 'this place' must be unmasked and clarified. I have argued elsewhere that the role of the theologian and intellectual as well as those we call 'poor' needs to move beyond the romantic descriptions we provide.[16] Majid's thesis forces us to consider the complexity of identities in post-conflict societies. Liberation biblical scholars wishing to ply their trade of liberation hermeneutics would also do well to move beyond fixed and stock descriptions and romantic notions of the poor and intellectuals.

Quoting Stuart Hall's work on identity, Majid says that identity is far from the simple thing we think it is (ourselves always in the same place). When understood correctly, it is always a split structure. It always features ambivalence. The story of identity is a cover story. A cover story for making you think that you have stayed in the same place, though with another bit of your mind you do know that you've moved on.[17]

Liberation theology has to be careful of the seeming wish of the dominant that identities should remain stable. Many years ago there was fierce debate within the African biblical hermeneutics session of the Society of Biblical Literature about the advisability of a session on HIV. The debate centred on the idea that HIV, as important as it was in our scholarship, should not become the defining identity of Africans within the academy. I recall a colleague saying that she did not wish to sing her sad songs in Babylon. Although you don't want to be robbed of your identity, you also do not want to be defined by it. The book invites us to consider the nuancing of identities, for the Moor is not some exotic dancing bear that we can pull out to represent the stable ahistorical figure of hegemonic discourses.

(c) Identification

The third eye/I of the Moor is the 'I' for identification. The most striking feature of Majid's book is the lines of identification drawn between the Moor expelled from Spain in the sixteenth and seventeenth centuries and the Moor re-emerging within discourses of immigration in the twenty-first century. How does prejudice manage to re-invent itself even within the most liberal societies?

The 're-invention' was clearly apparent in May 2014 in South Africa, when the Chief Justice of South Africa, Mogoeng Mogoeng, addressing a conference on law and religion in Stellenbosch, used the same text (Romans 13) used to justify apartheid rule to argue why religion needed to be infused into the Constitution in order to protect 'morality':

If a way could be found through legal mechanisms to elevate the role of love and the sensible discouragement of divorce, marital and family sanctity and stability would be enhanced. A legal framework that frowns upon adultery, fornication, separation and divorce, subject to appropriate modification, would, idealistic as this may appear to be, help us curb the murders that flow from adultery. It would reduce the number of broken families and the consequential lost and bitter generation that seems to be on the rise, and causes untold harm to society.[18]

The liberation movement in South Africa was deeply influenced and driven by theologians who aligned themselves with the central tenets of liberation theology. The joke made about liberation theology in Latin America can apply to South Africa. The joke in Latin America goes: 'Liberation theology made an option for the poor, but the poor made an option for Pentecostalism.' In South Africa, it can be said that liberation theology made an option for the oppressed and for the African National Congress, the ANC. The ANC, however, made an option for Pentecostalism. In other words, this brand of theology which the democratic ANC government has aligned itself with is not the theology used to fight apartheid theology: that is, a radical prophetic theology. Instead, the President, especially by his election of Chief Justice Mogoeng wa Mogoeng, has aligned himself with a religious right that wants to interpret the Constitution through their 'church theology'.

While many theologians have argued for liberation theology to be transformed into a theology of reconstruction in post-apartheid South Africa, I would argue that liberation hermeneutics first needs to re-claim a strong identification with the central tenets of liberation theology as a dominant theological paradigm. If this is not done, then the Moor will re-emerge, though with a different face.

Majid[19] captures this well: 'The more one thinks about the networked world we live in, the more difficult it is to believe that we can still inhabit the nations and adopt the ideologies bequeathed on the world by Spain in the sixteenth century.'

IV   Conclusion

I conclude with the words of the late Nelson Mandela: 'As religion fortified us in resisting oppression, we know that it can help strengthen us to carry out the mission that history has given to our generation and the next – to make a reality of our hopes for a better life for all.'[20] In order to harness the resources which religion offers us, we may need new I's/eyes for reading – perhaps the eyes of the Moor?

Notes

1. Sourced from Statistics South Africa.
2. Randall C. Bailey *et al.* (eds), *They Were All Together in One Place? Toward Minority Biblical Criticism*, Atlanta, 2009, p. 6.
3. Stephen Biko, *I write what I like*, London, 1978; *id.*, *Black Consciousness in South Africa*, Millard Arnold (ed.), New York, 1978.
4. Feminist epistemologies are primarily constructed by way of narrative rather than propositionally, hence the use of personal narrative as a methodology in this article. See Nadar (2014).
5. See 'Race, Equity, and Public Schools in Post-Apartheid South Africa: Is Opportunity Equal for All Kids?' by Yamauchi Futoshi, who concludes that 'opportunities for education in public schools are still unequal between black and white children in South Africa, even post-apartheid', http://www.ifpri.org/sites/default/files/publications/fcnbr182.pdf.
6. Anouar Majid, *We Are All Moors: Ending Centuries of Crusades against Muslims and Other Minorities*, Minneapolis, 2009, p. x.
7. *Ibid.*, p. 122.
8. Takatso A. Mofokeng, 'Black Christians, the Bible and Liberation', *Journal of Black Theology in South Africa* 1:2 (May 1988), pp. 34–42; and Itumeleng J. Mosala, *Biblical Hermeneutics and Black Theology in South Africa*, Grand Rapids, 1989.
9. Desmond M. Tutu, 'Liberation as a Biblical Theme', in *Hope and Suffering: Sermons and Speeches*, Grand Rapids, 1989, pp. 48–87; Allan A. Boesak, *Black and Reformed: Apartheid, Liberation, and the Calvinist Tradition*, Maryknoll, 1984.
10. Justin Ukpong, 'Developments in Biblical Interpretation in Africa: Historical and Hermeneutical Directions', in West & Dube (eds), *The Bible in Africa: Transactions, Trajectories and Trends*, Leiden, 2000, pp. 11–28, here at p. 19.
11. Kimberle Crenshaw, 'Demarginalizing the Intersection of Race and Sex: A Black Feminist Critique of Antidiscrimination Doctrine, Feminist Theory and Antiracist Politics', *University of Chicago Legal Forum*, vol. 1989, p. 139.
12. Patricia Hill Collins, *Black Feminist Thought: Knowledge, Consciousness, and the Politics of Empowerment*, 2nd ed., New York & London, 2000, p. 299.
13. Anouar Majid, *We Are All Moors, op. cit.*, p. 9.
14. Bailey *et al.*, *They Were All Together in One Place?*, p. 6.
15 Anouar Majid, *We Are All Moors, op. cit.*, p. 168.
16. *Cf.* Sarojini Nadar, 'Beyond the "ordinary reader" and the "invisible intellectual": Shifting Contextual Bible Study from Liberation Discourse to Liberation Pedagogy', *Old Testament Essays* 22:2 (2009), p. 388.
17. Anouar Majid, *We Are All Moors, op. cit.*, p. 168.
18. See Mogoeng wa Mogoeng, 'Law and Religion in Africa', in *The Quest for the Common Good in Pluralistic Societies*, http://www.justice.gov.za/ocj/speeches/20140527-Stellenbosch.pdf.
19. Anouar Majid, *We Are All Moors, op. cit.*, p. 168.
20. 'Mandela Speech at a Methodist Church Service in Langa', ANC, http://www.anc.org.za/ancdocs/history/mandela/1999/nm0213.html.

Religion as Social Capital for Building Peace

DANIEL FRANKLIN PILARIO

The article is about the idea of social capital as applied to religions in post-conflict societies, and draws on pastoral experiences in Southern Mindanao (the Philippines). In it I try to rethink the excessively optimistic concept of (religious) 'social capital' advanced by the Harvard-based political theorist, Robert Putnam, and by the World Bank, and describe its advantages and difficulties as they are played out in a long-standing Christian–Muslim conflict in Asia. I argue that experiences from the rough grounds can and do challenge dominant theories almost taken for granted by scholarly and scientific discourse. I also assess the repercussions of this theoretical tendency on theological thinking and pastoral practice.

I Social capital, religions and peace

The notion of social capital has become a well-known sociological category in the last two to three decades. At least in the English-speaking world, the concept of social capital has been popularized by Robert Putnam, a Harvard-based political scientist, with the publication of his book *Bowling Alone*.[1] In his analysis, American society has experienced a decline in social capital, as exemplified in people 'bowling alone' as opposed to previous lively competitions among neighbourhood leagues, usually after work. Social capital is defined as 'connections among individuals – social networks and norms of reciprocity and trustworthiness that arise from them'.[2] Putnam identifies two kinds of social capital: bonding social capital (exclusive social groupings by ethnicity, gender, religions, and so on); and bridging social capital (inclusive networks that cuts across social divides and link people from different genders, ages, races or classes). Regardless of type, however, what is important to Putnam is social capital's power to induce social cohesion, which makes his project a contemporary Durkheimian revival, as some social scientists call it.[3] The concept has gained ascendancy since it was also adopted by the World Bank, the Organization for Economic Cooperation and Development (OECD), and other international economico-political bodies. In the World Bank's view, social capital can be measured in the quality of a society's groups and networks, trust and solidarity, collective action and cooperation, social cohesion and inclusion, information and communication.[4] It assumes, following Putnam, that social capital enhances economic capital and sustainable social peace.

We should ask if religion or religious belonging is a form of social capital? Here I shall try to locate the question in the experiences of conflict and peace-building on the ground, and more specifically in Southern Mindanao, the Philippines, an area of the country that has experienced intermittent conflict for decades, and where three groups of peoples distinguished by different cultures, languages and religions are present: Muslim communities, Christian settlers and indigenous peoples. The Comprehensive Agreement on the Bangsamoro has just been signed at the time of writing (27 March 2014),[5] and is awaiting Congressional approval to become a law. This document on Muslim autonomy in Southern Philippines has been seen by many as the way to peace in this war-ravaged land. It is a product of 17 years of tedious negotiation and haggling, dialogue and reaching out, and prayer and fasting by all parties: government and warring factions, military and religious representatives, and NGOs and cultural communities.

At present, a study is still needed of the influence of religions on this peace-process.[6] I would group some initiatives known to me into three areas: (a) dialogue at 'official' levels; (b) dialogue at the grassroots; (c) peace education and theologies of peace.

II High-profile dialogues

Since the 1970s, and a highly-charged situation on the ground, dialogue and consultations initiated by religious leaders (bishops and *ulama*, pastors and imams, faith-based NGOs, and so on) have taken place at international, national and diocesan levels: 'Given the fact that these dialogues were organized and carried out in the midst of considerable tension and sometimes actual warfare between Christians and Muslims, they give evidence of considerable courage and vision in offering a serious alternative to increased polarization and conflict.'[7] The participants in these dialogues, that is, religious leaders of Muslim and Christian communities, gained some social capital by participating, as they were also involved in government consultations within the general peace process.

III Grassroots dialogue movements

Even if high-profile dialogue is properly documented, only a few people take part in these meetings. The agreements achieved remain at 'official' levels. Deep-seated prejudices persist on both sides. Christians see Muslims as 'traitors' and 'terrorists', and Muslims view Christians as land-grabbers and proselytizers. In the context of killings, bombings and kidnappings blamed on both sides, these biases are continually reproduced in people's minds and bodies. The real dialogue needs to happen among people in their everyday life. This trend is fostered and encouraged by people working at the grassroots: Christians and Muslims, church-based groups and NGOs. From the Christian side, parish priests, pastors, religious and lay leaders pursue a life of dialogue among Muslims through their pastoral services, which are accessible to all: for instance, education, health, housing, social services, cooperatives, and so on. This life of witness slowly invites a change of heart and mind among Muslims. A story is told of a group of Christians who just settled in Sitangkay, a small island occupied by a predominantly Muslim populace. They wanted to build a small chapel for themselves but met with vigorous resistance from the Muslim authorities and neighbourhood, until a local policeman, a Muslim, volunteered to intercede for them. He said he was once a student in a Catholic school of a nearby island, and he was not subjected to proselytizing. This small chapel still stands today.[8] From the Muslim side, I heard some real-life stories as I visited these small island communities. The week before I arrived, the Christians told me, the Muslim community had expelled their *tabligh* (or Muslim missionary) from their island for sowing prejudice against Christians. I surmised that the Christians told me this on my arrival in order to warn me: if you do the same, you will end up like him. On both sides, the faith resources of ordinary people on the ground have become a social capital for mutual existence and peace.

IV Peace education and peace theologies

I also encountered broad and more conscious initiatives to promote peace. For instance, Christian schools and madrassas integrate peace education into their curriculum, conduct common interfaith activities among students (retreats, youth camps, and so on). In places of intense conflict, the local populace (Muslims, Christians and indigenous peoples together) declare their places 'zones of peace', and prevent armed military groups from carrying firearms within the specified locality and, in some cases, designate women (some of them mothers) for peace-keeping. Specialized institutions promote theologies of dialogue with Muslim and Christian participants in live-in programmes. They study the Bible and Qur'an together, exploring the histories and spiritualities of both faiths, and immerse themselves among ordinary people.[9]

V Ambivalence and missing voices

There are ambivalences and missing voices, however, on this road to peace. Two of them are religiously-inspired separatist groups, and the silence of indigenous peoples. Some religiously-inspired groups do not hesitate to use violence to promote their causes. Islamic-inspired militant units of the Abu Sayyaf group, with its connection to the Al-Queda network, are fired up by radical interpretations of Islam, and intend to claim their ancestral lands from the Christians and establish a total Islamic State under Allah. These groups are not accepted by mainstream Muslims, but their continued use of violence has tarnished the peace process. On the Christian side, there are armed groups called '*Ilaga*' (the local word for 'rats'), who also refer to themselves as 'God's Army' or the 'Christian Militia'. With religious amulets, pictures of Christ or rosaries worn as necklaces hanging next to their firearms, they claim that no bullet can hit them, since they are protected by God as they in turn protect the Christian population from Muslim violence. These two groups and many others do not fit the all-optimistic view of religious social capital in Putnam's paradigm.

Another dimension is missing in the Southern Philippines: the voices of non-Islamized indigenous peoples. Before the coming of Islam and Christianity centuries ago, the entire Philippines was populated by diverse indigenous peoples with their own cultures, languages and religions. The majority were converted to Islam or to Christianity, but many people hold on to their indigenous cultures and beliefs; more than 2.1 million of them are in Mindanao. But they do not feature often in ongoing interreligious and political dialogue, which takes place mainly between two great religions with substantial social capital: Christianity and Islam. Where have all the indigenous religions gone? Now that the new autonomous government is about to be set up, indigenous people are afraid that they will be subsumed again in a dominant political and discursive formation. In the past it was by the Christians; now it will be by the Muslims.

VI   Rethinking religious social capital in peace-building

Three concluding theoretical considerations can be discerned in the above narratives from the ground: the ambivalence of religious social capital; the consequent need for an analysis of power; and sensitivity and engagement with silenced religious voices.

Religions are at best ambivalent as social capital for peace-building. Robert Putnam's and the World Bank's very optimistic assessments of (religious) social networks as crucial factors for the common good, alow us to assess what mainstream religions are doing, but do not take into account the ambivalence of exclusive intra-ethnic social and religious bonds (bonding social capital), and their propensity to marginalization.[10] As mainstream religions try to reach out, they also tend to exclude minorities (those outside the social-capital network). The counter-reaction of extremists and 'fundamentalists' can be explained as a consequence of this process of exclusion. Social networks (in our case, religious social networks), are most often subsumed in the word 'community', which is a favourite term of churches and religious groups, although (as Raymond Williams points out), it is also a difficult and complex word.[11] In the context of our discussion, 'community' has not only descriptive but exclusionary connotations (for instance, 'gated communities' or 'Christian community') that tend to expel 'the other' outside a bonded or bounded social network.

There is also a need for an analysis of power in the conceptualization of religious social capital. We might say that Putnam's Durkheimian revival needs Marx. Pierre Bourdieu, the French sociologist, also talks of social capital and social networks. But, in contradictinction to Putnam, Bourdieu thinks that social capital (because it can be translated into cultural and economic capital) tend to acquire them as part of a group's economic-political power.[12] In Bourdieu's critical view, those who know more (cultural and social capital) can have more (economic capital), and those who have more, always win the social game. Those who have less not only lag behind but are effectively expelled from the race. Now that the Muslims in the Philippines have 'more' (politically, economically, culturally and socially), they are listened to and are engaged with. Since the indigenous peoples do not have enough, they are forced to retreat inland, into the forests, to protect themselves from the crossfire of the dominant players. Without an analysis of power in the conception of social and religious capital, there is no end to this exclusionary social process.

A similar tendency appears in some un-nuanced Christian theologies of communion. There is an obvious example in a CDF document of 1992 which deplores the inadequate integration of the 'mystery of communion' in the concept of the People of God. The intention was to denigrate the 'merely sociological' dimension of the Church by enthroning the divine and mystical aspects of 'communion with God overflowing into communion among men [sic]'.[13] These attempts at dematerialization risk forgetting that the Church is also a human entity navigating in social space, which means that it has potential advantages but is also vulnerable to manipulation by those exerting power. In Joseph Komonchak's words: 'An ontology of the Church that neglects the human, history-shaped, and history-shaping element falls short of the properly theological meaning of the word "mystery". I think we still lack an ecclesiology adequate to *Lumen gentium* 8.'[14]

The third consideration is that of engagement with silenced and forgotten religious voices. We sometimes ignore the fact that these indigenous beliefs are also depositories of authentic desires for peace and human well-being. Although the Church treats other mainstream ancient faiths with respect, and engages them in dialogue (at least in its official statements), it hesitates to do so with followers of traditional religions and indigenous faiths whose dangers are already spelled out: '... inadequate ideas about God, superstition, fear of the spirits, objectionable moral practices, the rejection of twins (in some places), even occasional human sacrifice.' These are the words of a 1993 Vatican document on traditional religions.[15] Instead of dialogue, the document accords these religions no more than 'pastoral attention', as its title shows. Because of their weak social and cultural capital, indigenous religions are treated only with this kind of condescension.

Ironically (at least in my experience in the Philippines, beyond Christianity and Islam), these indigenous peoples' animistic religions are most intimately linked to the cosmos, most compassionate in human relations, and most sensitive to the divine. In short, they are most connected to peace.

Notes

1. Robert Putnam, *Bowling Alone: Collapse and Revival of American Community,* New York, 2000.

2. *Ibid.*, p. 19.

3. *Cf.* Anthony Elliott, *Contemporary Social Theory: An Introduction*, New York & London, 2014, p.

4. *Cf.* 'Understanding and Measuring Social Capital' at http://econ.worldbank.org; cf. Robert Putnam, 'Social Capital: Measurement and Consequences', at http://www1.oecd.org/edu/innovation-education/1825848.pdf.

5. 'Comprehensive Agreement on the Bangsamoro', http://www.gov.ph/2014/03/27/document-cab/.

6. For a good survey on Christian initiatives, see William LaRousse, *Walking Together Seeking Peace*, Quezon City, 2001, pp. 325–422.

6. *Ibid.*, p. 365.

8. *Ibid.*, p. 356.

9. Most popular is the Silsilah Dialogue Movement in Zamboanga City. *Cf.* http://www.silsilahdialogue.com/index.php/en/.

10. See, among others, Corwin Smidt (ed.), *Religion as Social Capital: Producing the Common Good*, Texas, 2003.

11. *Cf.* Raymond Williams, 'The Importance of Community', in *id.*, *Resources of Hope*, London, 1989, pp. 111–19.

12. Pierre Bourdieu, 'The Forms of Capital', in *Handbook of Theory and Research for the Sociology of Education*, John Richardson (ed.), New York, 1986, pp. 241–58.

13. Congregation of the Doctrine of Faith, 'Letter to the Bishops of the Catholic Church on some Aspects of the Church Understood as Communion', at http://www.vatican.va/roman_curia/congregations/cfaith/documents/rc_con_cfaith_doc_28051992_communionis-notio_en.html.

14. Joseph Komonchak, 'The Ecclesiology of Vatican II', http://publicaffairs.cua.edu/RDSpeeches/99Ecclesiology.cfm.

15. Pontifical Council for Interreligious Dialogue, 'Pastoral Attention to Traditional Religions', http://www.vatican.va/roman_curia/pontifical_councils/interelg/documents/rc_pc_interelg_doc_21111993_trad-relig_en.html.

Faith as Spiritual Capital

PERO SUDAR

Considered as the fundamental elements of Christian anthropology, revelation and Christian theology mediate and explain God as the One who loves humans and preserves their freedom and peace. Authentic faith in God, who made and loves all humankind, necessarily excludes violence. Furthermore, in spite of all false human ideas and historical prejudices, any genuine human faith in God also inspires human and neighbourly relations. True belief in God also enables his followers to see and understand people in mind and spirit as if through God's eyes, and the basic convictions of all forms of belief tend in that direction. To a great extent, the credibility of what the Churches and faith communities say about God and the eschatological goal of humanity depends on the strength of their mutual recognition and of their common commitment to the cause of peace as the paramount individual and general human value.

I Introduction

It was an extremely good idea to hold a conference on what is unfortunately still a very relevant topic, especially here in Sarajevo in 2014, with all its historical echoes. The fact that, in spite of so much tragically emphatic evidence buried somewhere deep in the darker areas of the human unconscious, the belief should have endured that it is still possible to use wars to resolve disputes between individuals and communities, means that we still have no alternative to study and discussion of violence as a godless and inhuman phenomenon.[1]

Here I shall concern myself primarily with the Christian theological origins of the irrefragable relation between faith and peace, and thus with the Churches' duty of commitment to non-violence. I would remark that my recourse to Christian theology in this regard is a result of my inadequate knowledge of the peace theology of other denominations, and does not reflect any kind of critical view of them.

II   Peace as God's gift and commission

Christian theology tells us that belief in God as the universal Creator is essential to the beneficent relationship between God and humankind, which in principle excludes violence and war as the culmination of the use of force.[2] The Bible informs us very convincingly of the indissoluble logical bond between the act of creation and God's love of what he has made. Since God in himself is the fullness of being and of all perfection, it accords with his nature that nothing compelled him to create the world. After all, he lacks nothing. Therefore we must suppose that God's love for life in general, and for people in particular, must be the sole ground for the creation. In this context, it is understandable that God fundamentally affirms and renews his loving-kindness towards humans in everything that he has already created and in everything that he continues to create.[3]

Christian theology recognizes the sublime truth that the glory of God is revealed in human life, and that human life is perception of God.[4] Since peace is both the framework and the basic prerequisite for the maintenance and development of life, it is not only possible but necessary to ensure that God's relationship with humans is interfused with peace. Peace is not merely the framework for the preservation of human life, and of all creation, but one of the conditions for the expression of God's love for human beings. Accordingly, we should think of peace as an integral part of the life that God has given us, and consequently as an essential element of faith. Christians acknowledge that God alone is peace.[5] They recognize Christ as the one who the prophets foretold would bring peace on earth,[6] and who himself is simultaneously peace[7] and peacemaker.[8]

But that is not all there is to the Christian theology of peace. Christ enjoined on all those who believe in him the duty of working for peace and reconciliation,[9] and made peace the prerequisite for the most sacred, that is, Eucharistic, form of communion and community with him. He even made the mere possibility of a relation between a believer and God dependent on the quality of relations between human beings.[10] Jesus made reconciliation between people a prerequisite for prayers to be answered[11] and for God's forgiveness.[12] Alongside the commandment to love our enemies,[13] this is certainly the most difficult injunction among the teachings of Jesus.

Of course, we have to ask why Jesus, who was otherwise so full of understanding for sinners and for human weaknesses, was so demanding when it came to forgiveness and reconciliation, which we humans find so difficult. Not infrequently, we find a readiness to be reconciled and to forgive tantamount to acceptance of injustice, and of a certain degree of personal and collective subservience. But, as history shows, there is no answer to this question other than the fact that it is difficult if not impossible to obtain peace without readiness for forgiveness and reconciliation. In the world of unjust people in which we live, the call for justice as the exclusive prerequisite for forgiveness and reconciliation merely reinforces the vicious circle in which force constantly gives rise to new force. Believers do not surrender their right to justice if they are prepared to ask for forgiveness or to offer it as a prerequisite for reconciliation. Instead, they prepare the way for the rule of justice. In fact, reaching the conviction that there is no way to peace without forgiveness, and no way to justice without peace, is a painful experience. But it is the prerequisite for ensuring that what makes human beings images of God in their innermost selves (that without which they would cease to be human) can endure.

Genuine faith in God also compels believers to ensure that the realization of their wishes, or of their missionary enthusiasm (they are sure that everyone should believe in God), should conform to the divine mode of action. That always has been and remains the great dilemma and major temptation for believers throughout history. The only solution is to be found in a consistent interpretation of the divine relationship with humans and with human freedom, and in firm attachment to human logic as a gift of God. Faith assumes God's omnipotence. If God wanted everyone to believe in him and to proclaim that belief in exactly the same way, he could make it happen. If almighty God decides not to have recourse to his power,[14] and clearly forces no one to believe in him, he must have a very compelling divine reason for this. This reason is his love for humankind, which is evident in the preservation of that freedom. It is precisely in this very relation of God to humans that believers must look for their inspiration for a peace-loving relationship with people, because they are human. It is also important to stress that the unconditional exercise of peace (not only because of its roots but because of its significance and range, because it directly affects the relationship between God and humankind) forms part of transcendent reality. A blessing used by Jesus took the following form: 'Blessed are the peacemakers, for they will be called the children of God', and he applied it to all those who, irrespective of their motives, really worked to establish peace among humans.[15] If faith in God is the inexhaustible source of inspiration by which people are conceived of, accepted and promoted as God's free creatures, then the pursuit of peace is one of the main duties of believers.

III   Moral imperative

Since faith is inseparably bound up in the human heart with the duty of promoting and extending goodness in people and between them,[16] the fact that an impermissibly large number of wars throughout history also had a religious connotation, will be seen to be inconceivable and incomprehensible.[17] In fact, only a few wars can really be called wars of religion, but there is reason to suppose that an even smaller number of wars were totally free from any admixture of religious motives. The followers of Jesus Christ must be ashamed to acknowledge[18] that even the second millennium has featured three wars with a high degree of denominational motivation, in which the number of people who died may be estimated as at least six million, and at most 24 million. With regard to our understanding of God as the Creator of humankind, which is common to all world religions and is especially important to the Abrahamitic religions, it should be emphasized that there is no more obvious and godless expression of unbelief than an attempt to use force to defend God from the human freedom to believe or not to believe. Believers can defend the truth about God only if they practise genuine love of humanity. In spite of this evident fact, throughout the history of the relevant religions they have never succeeded in resisting the temptation to use violent methods to defend and extend themselves. In fact, the contrary is true.[19]

It seems less difficult to cite the reasons why faith (which is inherently an inexhaustible source for the advocacy of peace) has been misused as inspiration for intolerance and conflicts between people, than to list ways of shielding faith from that kind of abuse. It appears that intolerance on the part of believers originates in and derives its motivation from two facts. The first is that the majority of believers do not know, or do not accept, the fundamental truths of their own faith. Believers who do not know their faith are very dangerous, since they can easily be persuaded to defend and spread their faith with means that are actually irreconcilable with it.

It is even easier to persuade them in the name of their beliefs to fight for interests that have nothing in common with faith.[20]

The second source of intolerance is concealed in the human longing for power, which is long-lasting and difficult to resist, and in the temptation to subject religion as well to this purely mundane inclination which is so contrary to faith. This assumption supports the fact that there has never been any lack of leaders and representatives of the Church and of religious communities who have succumbed to the temptation to use religion and the religious feelings of believers to achieve worldly and all too human aims. It is easy to disguise their unrestrained yearning for their own elevation and power as commitment to the greatness and power of their Church or community of faith, with which they identify as their 'own' cause.[21] This leads them ineluctably towards a 'misuse of dialogue with the socio-cultural structures of this world',[22] in which the authentic, humanitarian and consequently peace-loving power of faith is dispersed.

What is more, the major world religions, especially those so interwoven with their Abrahamitic roots, are not only fundamentally directed to human ends, but tend to inherit the theological emphases of mutual exclusion even to the point of intolerance and conflicts. On the one hand, they are similar with regard to origin and the roots from which they have developed, even to the point of a possible equal status. On the other hand, their theological and eschatological tendency (and consequently also their historical behaviour towards each other) makes them distinct even to the point of opposition. But God revealed the truth that he not only accepts humans but is emphatically and seriously focussed on all human beings precisely because they are human.[23] By reason of his relationship with humankind (which should be a secondary yet fundamental reason for the existence and effective operation of all faiths and all religions), this God of rejoicing and commitment necessarily gives rise to the moral duty of genuine reciprocal acceptance and respect between modes of belief and religions. That is the basic prerequisite not only for their fruitful cooperation in constructing a peace-loving world, but for the credible proclamation of the existence of God and of the human existential need to believe in God.

IV   Conclusion

The context of this article and the available space have not allowed me to deal with the full range of relevant theological and moral arguments, which would have enabled me to show all the more convincingly that faith is an inexhaustible source of strength and motivation that not only dissuades people from committing acts of violence, but turns them into convinced peacemakers. It is difficult to believe that peace and a life worthy of human beings would be possible somewhere on earth if it were not for the human emphasis on heaven. In fact, no one should call on and encourage people to direct their conduct on earth with reference to heaven, without first doing everything possible to reduce the obstacles that result from injustice. It is in this respect especially that religious communities demonstrate and prove the credibility of their talk of heaven. This applies especially to Bosnian-Herzegovinian society devastated by the cruelty of war and degraded by post-war injustice.

Translated by J. G. Cumming

Notes

1. It is calculated that 100,100,000 human lives were sacrificed in World Wars I and II and their immediate sequels. *Cf.* C. Smith, *Samoubojstvo Zapada*, Zagreb, 2007, p. 27. Currently nine wars are being waged in the world apart from the Ukraine. At least 1,000 people per year die in each of these wars. If we added those who have died among the consequential losses of all these wars, the total would be more horrific than the word 'horrific' could ever convey.
2. *Cf.* Gen. 1.1.
3. *Cf.* Gen. 28–30.
4. 'Gloria enim Dei vivens homo, vita autem hominis visio Dei.' Irenaeus, *Adversus Haereses* (Against Heresies) IV.XX.7. Variously translated, e.g.: 'The glory of God is the living human being; the life of a human being is the vision of God.'; 'The glory of God is a living human, and human life consists in beholding God.'; 'Life in humans is the glory of God; the life of humans is the vision of God.'; 'In the life of the man Jesus, the faithful behold the glory of God shining on the face of his Son.' A popular, though inaccurate, rendering, is: 'the glory of God is the human being fully alive…'.
5. 'Gideon built an altar there to the Lord and named it "The Lord is Peace"', Judges 6.24
6. 'For a child has been born to us, a son is given to us. He will bear the symbol of dominion on his shoulder, and his title will be: Wonderful Counsellor, Mighty Hero, Eternal father, Prince of Peace. Wide will be his dominion and boundless the peace bestowed on David's throne and on his kingdom, to establish and support it with justice and righteousness from now on, for evermore.' Isa. 9. 6–7. 'They will enjoy security, for then his greatness will reach to the ends of the earth. Then there will be peace.' Micah 5.4.
7. 'For Christ is our living peace.' Eph. 2.14; 'The God of peace be with you all, amen.' Rom. 15.33.
8. 'Then he came and told both you who were far from God and us who were near that the war was over.' Eph. 2.17; 'I leave behind with you—peace; I give you my own peace and my gift is nothing like the peace of this world. You must not be distressed and you must not be daunted.' John 14.27.
9. 'All this is God's doing, for he has reconciled us to himself through Jesus Christ; and he has made us agents of the reconciliation.' 2 Cor. 5.18. 'Finally, then, my brothers, cheer up!

Straighten yourselves out, comfort yourselves, agree with one another and live at peace. So shall the God of love and peace be ever with you.' 2 Cor. 13.11.

10. *Cf.* Matt. 5.23–4.

11. *Cf.* Mark 11.25.

12. Matt. 5.15.

13. 'You have heard that it used to be said "Thou shalt love thy neighbour and hate thine enemy". But I tell you, Love your enemies, and pray for those who persecute you, so that you may be sons of your Heavenly Father.' Matt. 5.43–5.

14. 'Almighty God crucified his omnipotence in Jesus Christ in order to tell all people of all ages that he loves them and that they are worthy of his concern.' P. Bosmans, *Taj nevjerojatni Bog*, Zagreb, 1989, p. 67.

15. Matt. 5.9.

16. See Tenzin Gyatso, the fourteenth Dalai Lama, on non-violence as an appropriate response to human conflict, *Concilium* 2003/5.

17. See Karl-Josef Kuschel, *Od sporenja k natjecanju religija*, Sarajevo & Zagreb, 2003.

18. *Cf. Il ghetto di Roma nel cinquecento*, Rome, 2014.

19. *Cf.* M. Jordan, *U ime Božje – nasilje i razaranje u svjetskim religijama*, Zagreb, 2008.

20. 'People thought that they could do the most ghastly things in your name. They besmirched your name throughout the centuries and made it a curse for their brothers.' P. Bosmans, *Taj nevjerojatni Bog, op. cit.*, p. 19.

21. F. Kamphaus, *Lichtblicke*, Freiburg im Breisgau, 2001, p. 167.

22. Jorge Mario Bergoglio, *La croce e la pace*, Bologna, 2014, p. 58.

23. 'But the Lord said, "You are sorry about the gourd, though you did not have the trouble of growing it, a plant which came up one night and died the next. And should I not be sorry about the great city of Niniveh, with its hundred and twenty thousand people who cannot tell their right hand from their left, as well as cattle without number?"' Jonah 4.10–11.

Part Four: United Europe: An Unfinished Project

Holy Lands and Sacred Nations

PANTELIS KALAITZIDIS

The confusion between religious and national identity, and the use of religion as an identity formation process, as well as the ethnic, racial, or religious conflicts we see in many settings (as, for instance, in the Balkans), are related to a very important and serious phenomenon: the claim of territorial exclusivity, and the consequent quest for a nationally, racially, and religiously 'pure' country, which is very often accompanied by a theology of self-justification and spiritual self-sufficiency, and the exaltation of collective egoisms. This idolization of religion, tribe, and nation, this odd paganism of earth, soil, and homeland, seems to be a real temptation for many Christian, and particularly Orthodox peoples, who, due to their painful historical experiences, often need to identify Church and nation. In this article, I intend to offer a theological critique of these phenomena, based on evidence from the Bible, patristics and contemporary theology and philosophy, and to address the challenges that our post-modern pluralistic societies pose to Christian faith and consciousness.

I Introduction

The confusion between religious and national identity that we see in many settings is related to a very important and serious phenomenon: the claim of territorial exclusivity. Indeed there doesn't seem to be an ethnic, racial, or religious conflict which does not include the claims of territorial exclusivity. Where, however, can we find a country that is nationally, racially, religiously, and linguistically unmixed? And what solution can be found when my city is also the city of 'the other', my country is the country of 'the other' – when the territories I claim to be mine in the name of my history or my religion are at the same time his or hers? Are nationalism, irredentism, pogroms, national homogenization, and religious or so-called 'patriotic' and 'defensive' wars the solution?

115

II   Land and exclusivity

It is equally difficult to imagine ethnic and religious conflicts without an ideology or even a theology of self-justification, without a mentality of spiritual self-sufficiency and introversion, without the cultivation of national pride, the worship of ancestors and exclusivity – all of which lead, very often, to a lack of tolerance toward what is different and to all kinds of ethnic cleansings and conflicts. Yet, wherever we have a prevalence of the spirit of self-sufficiency and self-justification, wherever stereotypes thrive regarding homeland, religion, tribe, and nation, wherever we have a predominance of praise for the achievements and virtues of our ancestors, wherever, finally, various forms of collective egoism, such as nationalism, find refuge – here, then, is the exact place where repentance and self-criticism will be absent; here is where the existential window that makes room for any kind of 'other' or 'stranger', any kind of fellow human being, our neighbour – who is in the image of the 'Other' and 'Stranger' par excellence – becomes an elusive dream. And, as we can easily understand, without repentance we can neither have forgiveness nor can we speak of reconciliation. If we consider war, violence, all kind of conflicts, even those taking place in the name of religion, from a spiritual point of view, in the end, they are nothing but the result of the exaltation of collective egoisms; they only witness to the absence of real repentance, the denial of the spirit of the Cross. Behind any conflict, we can easily discern an idolization of religion, tribe, and nation, an odd paganism of earth, soil, and homeland, or of the 'God-bearing' people and its claim to exclusivity, which is a real temptation.[1]

Precisely this connection of geographical land and national or religious exclusivity is marvellously analyzed by the French philosopher Régis Debray in a paragraph of his *God, An Itinerary*,[2] bearing this descriptive title: "we are all mammals", since the claim of this kind of exclusivity is brilliantly parallellized by Debray with the practice of mammals who are trying, through urination, to define, 'describe' and ensure the place they wish to occupy and control exclusively. Yet, as we are reminded by Debray, with the advent of Christianity, terms and realities such as 'promised land', 'holy lands', 'holy city' and so on, are losing their significance.

For example, Paul's letters do not refer, nor are they addressed, to some 'promised land' or some specific 'homeland,' but to the whole world. We can also, according to Debray, recall the beginning of John's gospel: The Word became flesh and dwelt among us' (John 1.14). Even if we know the historical and geographical location of the Incarnation, we are unable to define exactly 'where' he 'dwelt among us', because no form of attachment to the land, no metaphysical way of being confined to the land or the homeland, can find a place in the perspective inaugurated by Christianity. The eschatological and migratory character of Christian existence,[3] this sense of emigration and ephemerality that living according to and in Christ entails, makes the Church a people en route, journeying within history without being established in history (and geography). The Christian life is one of journey and constant movement, imitating in this way the journey and emigration of Abraham, the patriarch of faith who had to abandon his homeland and emigrate away from his land in order to respond to God's call and make a covenant with him.[4] According to Debray: 'The Christian is a person marching ahead, not remaining "within", but this journey, when it is faithful to the fundamental characteristics of Christianity, is not in relation to some geographical centre. The body of Christ is now the centre, and not "the holy land" or any earthly homelands. This charismatic body is therefore the real territory and the real sanctuary of Christian, the new "land of promise", its new homeland.'[5]

Of course, one could argue that this is an approach influenced by Protestant theology and practice, which rejects, among other things, pilgrimage, holy relics and 'holy geography', as Debray himself partly claims.[6] Yet this is a very hasty approach that ignores the deeper sense of Orthodox Christianity and its authentic liturgical tradition. Even one of the great Cappadocian Fathers, Gregory of Nyssa, sharply criticized and challenged the custom, already established in the fourth century, of a 'religious' pilgrimage to the places where Jesus Christ was born and lived, that is, the very concept of the 'Holy Land', recalling instead that 'when the Lord invites the blessed to their inheritance in the kingdom of heaven, He does not include a pilgrimage to Jerusalem amongst their good deeds; when he announces the Beatitudes, He does not name amongst them that sort of devotion.'[7]

Fr. Alexander Schmemann, perhaps the greatest Orthodox liturgical scholar of the twentieth century, brilliantly explicated this same critical view regarding 'holy land' from a eucharistic/eschatological perspective – without, however, neglecting the historical and patristic foundations –, and is not remiss in recalling the practice of the ancient Church: 'Early Christians had no concern for any sacred geography, no temples ... There was no specific religious interest in the places where Jesus had lived. There

117

were no pilgrimages. The old religion had its thousand sacred places and temples: for the Christians all this was past and gone. There was no need for temples built of stone: Christ's Body, the Church itself, the new people gathered in Him, was the only real temple. ... The Church itself was the new and heavenly Jerusalem: the Church in Jerusalem was by contrast unimportant. The fact that Christ comes and is present was far more significant than the places where He had been. The historical reality of Christ was of course the undisputed ground of the early Christians' faith: yet they did not so much remember Him as know He was with them.'[8]

III   Spiritual homeland

This paradoxical and antinomic position of Christians in the world, which could be called 'a unique Christian eschatological anarchism', is what differentiates them from the world, the forms and the powers of this century, without leading them to a denial of the world. This eschatologically inspired distance-keeping keeps them from being identified with a particular nation, culture or even from dealing with national-identity issues. As 1 Peter shows us, for instance (2.9), there was a strong feeling that Christians understood themselves as a distinct nation, the new Israel, the new people of God, the third race, neither Jews nor Greeks. As the pre-eminent Russian diaspora theologian Fr. Georges Florovsky notes: 'There is, after Christ, but one "nation," the Christian nation, *genus Christianum* ... i.e. precisely the Church, the only people of God, and no other national description can claim any further Scriptural warrant: national differences belong to the order of nature and are irrelevant in the order of grace.'[9]

This 'race' of Christians is not based on racial or ethnic criteria, but on faith in Jesus Christ. It is not determined by differences according to birth in the flesh, but by the unity that is granted by spiritual birth in Christ. Its mission is to embrace all humanity, all nations, in accordance with the concluding words of the gospel of Matthew: 'Go therefore and make disciples of all nations, baptizing them in the name of the Father and of the Son and of the Holy Spirit.'[10]

In this perspective, the Church is seen as a spiritual homeland, a spiritual genus, in which all the divisions of nature (race, language, culture, genus, gender, social class) are overcome and the mystery of unity in Christ and the fellowship of divided humanity unfold. The Church is a new people, a new nation, which is not identified with any other people, race or earthly nation, since what characterizes it is not blood ties or subjection to the natural state of affairs, but the voluntary personal response to the call of God and the free participation in the Body of Christ and the life of grace.[11]

Doesn't all this necessitate the relativization of the concepts of nation and earthly homeland? If the Church, 'through ... the abundance of grace and the free gift',[12] is a spiritual genus and a spiritual homeland, can it at the same time be identified with a nation, serving the objectives and goals of the earthly, worldly homeland? And as legitimate as these goals may be, can they serve as the core of the ecclesiastical kerygma, replacing and marginalizing the essential and primary elements of the Church – above all, the eschatological dimension? Perhaps the eschatological dimension diminishes and relativizes otherwise legitimate patriotism – the interest in nations and homelands according to the flesh – precisely because eschatology establishes another measure of evaluation.

Isn't this the spirit of what St Gregory of Nazianzus maintained when he gave voice to the Church's eschatological conscience, relativizing the earthly homeland, as well as the other worldly values, and even going so far as to assure us that 'there is one country for those of lofty character, the Jerusalem of the mind, not these earthly nations set apart in their little borders with their many changing inhabitants'?[13]

IV Local and catholic

Contemporary Orthodox rhetoric is, however, characterized by a fundamental contradiction, by a tragic misunderstanding concerning the meaning of the involvement of Church and theology in history or even the Incarnation of Truth within history. Involvement in history is usually related to the struggle for the nation and identification with its culture. Thus (in order to focus on a single example), whenever the official ecclesiastical discourse speaks against globalization or calls for resistance to globalization, the Church does not invoke theological arguments or criteria but cultural and national ones, arguments about the defence of national independence, and about language and identity being in danger. However, it neglects to point out the negative financial and social consequences of globalization for the poor and the marginalized. What happens here is the complete inversion of the criteria of the Gospel: the defence of the poor, which was a priority in Christ's teaching,[14] recedes, and its place is taken by the defence of the endangered national and cultural identity.

Therefore, the principle of the local church, fundamental for Orthodox theology and ecclesiology, should not degenerate, as often happens today, by the consecration and sacralization of all kinds of localism, particularism and nationalism. All local churches are called to disclose the fullness of life they experience, the catholicity of the truth that they experience and that leads us to true ecumenism. And this catholicity unavoidably means the relativization of any partiality, any reality dividing unity, any reality which is destined to be surmounted in the eschaton, such as tribe, nation, location, etc.[15] As the Metropolitan of Pergamon, John D. Zizioulas, puts it: 'But a local Church is a strictly geographical concept and must not be understood in a phyletistic way; it is even meant to contradict and exclude phyletism. The geographical or better territorial principle in ecclesiology implies that in a local Church all divisions, natural, social, cultural etc., are transcended in the one body of Christ. Just as there will be 'neither Jew nor Greek' in the Kingdom, in the same way the local church is meant to include in it all nationalities, races etc that happen to live in that place. … Nationalism, when it becomes the basic ingredient of the concept of the local church is contrary to this principle of ecclesiology.'[16]

Even though the preaching of the Gospel is addressed to all nations,[17] the acceptance of this preaching and incorporation into the ecclesiastical body does not happen on the basis of the collectives of the people and the nation, but on the basis of a completely personal action, independent of any biological, cultural or national definitions. This is what is so radically new about the ecclesial way of life: it conveys God's personal call for a meeting and a relationship with him, through Jesus Christ, as well as the response to this call, which is also personal. After the dozens of works that have been written about the theology of person, it is unnecessary for me to belabour the fact that personal does not mean individual, but nor does it mean collective; for the personal call and the response to this call are not institutional, nor a product of individualism or collectivism, but rather of an ecclesial communion of persons, a communion of saints. The call that Christ addresses to us is personal and is not addressed to some collective of nation, race, people, and so on. The call of the twelve,[18] Paul's conversion on the road to Damascus,[19] the parable of the Good Samaritan,[20] Jesus' encounter with Zacchaeus,[21] the Canaanite woman,[22] the Roman centurion,[23] or even the Samaritan woman at Jacob's well[24] (to ground this argument in a few specific biblical examples), are not only absolutely personal events and choices that are not mediated by religious, national, linguistic, cultural or class collectives, but very often personal choices that are turned against the particular collectives or that push against the framework and limits that they have laid out. The collective of the nation does not take shape in the New Testament, not because some supposedly private religiosity or individual version of faith and salvation arose then, but because the only collective that is recognized is the Church – the new people of God – which is, however, a spiritual 'race'. This new people is formed, therefore, not on the basis of race, nation, language or culture, but on the basis of admission into the Body of Christ, offering universality and catholicity.

V Conclusion

The Orthodox as well as Christians from other traditions will urgently have to decide which of these two we support and profess: the unity of all and the universal brotherhood of humans, or national particularity? In the time and in the context of a multinational pluralistic post-modern society, Christianity loses the theological and spiritual resources of the biblical, patristic and Eucharistic tradition in the rhetoric of 'identities' and in an outdated religious tribalism. At the same time the insistence of many Greek Orthodox clerics and lay people – as well as of Orthodox from other churches or countries – on seeing Orthodoxy as a part of the national identity and culture, related to ancestral customs and traditional folklore, undermines every serious attempt to face the challenges that the contemporary world poses to Orthodoxy, and condemns the latter to continue to be trapped in traditionalism, fundamentalism, social anachronism, pre-modernity and the authoritarian structures of patriarchal society. As a result, along with ideological constructions such as 'Helleno-Christianity' (or the 'Holy Russia-Third Rome', the 'Christian Kingdom of Serbia and the Serbian people as servant of God', 'the Latin character and uniqueness of Romanian Orthodoxy', and so on, to recall some other examples), theocracy and neo-nationalism – which are presumably nothing other than secularized forms of eschatology – represent the dominant political vision of Eastern Christianity.

Meanwhile, Eastern Christianity continues to long for a romantic version of 'Christian' society and to dream of the forms and schemes of the

Constantinian era. Nowadays, in the era of globalization, when national identities are challenged by this supranational project, the old dilemma: catholicity or particularism, universality or locality, rises again, and asks for an open discussion in the Churches. The relationship between Christian identity and national identity, and the subsequent claims of territorial exclusiveness are in the heart of this discussion, while our capacity for forgiveness, reconciliation, peace, and peaceful coexistence is to a great extent dependent on the answer we shall give to it.

Notes

1. Matt. 28.19.
2. See more on this in P. Kalaitzidis & N. Asproulis, 'Greek Religious Nationalism Facing the Challenges of Evangelization, Forgiveness, and Reconciliation', in Semegnish Asfaw, Alexios Chehadeh & Marian G. Simion (eds), *Just Peace: Orthodox Perspectives*, Geneva, 2012, pp. 68–89. On the connection between religion, ethnicity, national identity and the idea of a 'chosen people' and its impact on the issues of violence and fundamentalism, see C. C. O'Brien, *God Land: Reflections on Religion and Nationalism*, Cambridge, MA. & London, 1988; M. E. Marty & R. S. Appleby (eds), *Religion, Ethnicity, and Self-Identity: Nations in Turmoil*, Hanover & London, 1997; R. S. Appleby, *The Ambivalence of the Sacred: Religion, Violence, and Reconciliation*, Lanham, MD, 2000; T. Meyer, *Identity Mania: Fundamentalism and Politicization of Cultural Differences*, London & New York, 1997; A. D. Smith, *Chosen Peoples: Sacred Sources of National Identity*, Oxford, 2003.
3. R. Debray, *Dieu, un itinéraire*, Paris, 2003, pp. 147ff.; *cf.* pp. 139–142.
4. See Hebr. 13.14.
5. See Gen. 12.
6. R. Debray, *Dieu, un itinéraire, op. cit.*, pp. 195–6.
7. *Ibid.*, p. 142.
8. Gregory of Nyssa, Letter 2: On Pilgrimages to Jerusalem, *PG* 46, 1009C; *cf.* 1012D, 1015C–1016A. (ET by William Moore & Henry Austin Wilson, *Nicene and Post-Nicene Fathers, Second Series, vol. 5*, Philip Schaff & Henry Wace (eds), Edinburgh, 1892, pp. 42–3).
9. Fr Alexander Schmemann, *For the Life of the World*, Crestwood, NY, 2002, p. 20.
10. G. Florovsky, 'Revelation and Interpretation', in *Bible, Church, Tradition: An Eastern Orthodox View*, vol. I in the *Collected Works of G. Florovsky*, Belmont, MA, 1972, p. 35.
11. *Cf.* G. Florovsky, 'On the Veneration of Saints', in *Creation and Redemption*, vol. III in the *Collected Works of G. Florovsky*, Belmont, MA, 1976, pp. 201–2: 'In Holy Christening the one to be enlightened leaves this world, and forsakes its vanity, as if freeing himself and stepping out of the natural order of things; from the order of "flesh and blood" one enters an order of grace. All inherited ties and all ties of blood are severed. But man is not left solitary or alone. For according to the expression of the Apostle "by one Spirit are we all baptized," neither Scythians nor Barbarians—and this nation does not spring through a relationship of blood but through freedom into one Body.'
12. Rom. 5.17.
13. Gregory of Nazianzus, Oration 24, *PG* 35, 1188AB (ET from *St Gregory of Nazianzus: Select Orations*, The Fathers of the Church series, vol. 107, ET by Martha Vinson,

Washington, DC, 2003, p.152). *Cf. id.*, 'Against the Arians, and Concerning Himself' (Oration 33), *PG* 36, 229A.

14. See Matt. 25. 40. See also Berdyaev's aphorism: 'The question of bread for myself is a material question, but the question of bread for my neighbours, for everybody, is a spiritual and a religious question.' in N. Berdyaev, *The Origin of Russian Communism*, ET by R. M. French, Ann Arbor, MI, 1960, p. 185. *Cf. id.*, *The Destiny of Man*, ET by Natalie Duddington, San Rafael, CA, 2009 (Greek tr. by Evtychia B. Gioultsis, Thessaloniki, 1980, p.135).

15. For an analysis in depth, *cf.* P. Kalaitzidis, 'The Church and the Nation in Eschatological Perspective', in P. Kalaitzidis, *The Church and Eschatology, The 2000–01 Volos Academy Winter Programme*, Athens, 2003, pp. 339–73 (in Greek; ET by Fr. Gregory Edwards forthcoming from WCC Publications, Geneva).

16 J. D. Zizioulas, 'Church Unity and the Host of Nations', in K. C. Felmy (ed.), *Kirchen im Kontext unterschiedlicher Kulturen: Auf dem Weg ins dritte Jahrtausend*, Göttingen, 1991, p.101.

17. See Matt. 24.14, 28.19–20; Mark 13.10; Luke 24.47.

18. *Cf.* Matt. 4.18–22; 10.1–4; Mark 1.16–20; 3.13–9; Luke 5.1–11; 6.12–6.

19. *Cf.* Acts 9.1–19. *Cf.* also Acts 22.6–16; 26.12–8.

20. Luke 10.25–37.

21. Luke 19.1–10.

22. Matt. 15.21–8; Mark 7.24–30.

23. Matt. 8.5–13; Luke 7.1–10; John 4.43–54.

24. John 4.4–42.

What Does It Mean To Be A European Muslim?

DŽEVAD HODŽIĆ

The future of humankind will depend largely on relations between world religions. The situation of Muslims in modern West European societies is even more significant when viewed in this context, and is governed to a considerable extent by how Muslims see themselves. This article covers the following major features of the modern self-understanding of Muslims in Europe and with regard to the politico-legal and cultural context of their presence there: the original Islamic concept of religion, the Muslim attitude to modernity, the constitutive implications of interreligious dialogue for Islamic revelation and the modern Islamic identity in Europe, inclusive Islamic theology, and Islamic thought and education in the languages of the third generation of Muslim Europeans. The European Islamic identity requires a self-critical approach, dialogue, movement and open-mindedness within the framework of the foregoing reference variables.

I Muslim identity

From the historical perspective of the West, the main characteristic of the Islamic identity is that it is different. From this viewpoint, in the past it has been assumed, and is still generally taken to be the case today, that being a Muslim means being an outsider or foreigner, someone different. Grounded and established as it was on a hegemonic basis, Western Orientalism conceived of the East in general, and accordingly the adherents of Islam, as other or others. 'Orientalism is more credible as an indicator for a Euro-Atlantic superiority vis-à-vis the East than as a potential source of credible statements about the East.'[1] Western discourse about Islam as influenced by Orientalism inclines to the historically unjustifiable 'thesis of the exclusively Christian, monocultural, monolithic nature of European culture',[2] and therefore to a thesis which completely ignores 'the strong presence and determinative influence of Islam on the formation of the political, economic, cultural and spiritual identity of Europe'.[3]

In addition to the long historical presence of Muslims on the continent of Europe, since the second half of the twentieth century millions of Muslims have also been living in Western and Northern European countries. These Muslim communities strive to obtain their own space, rights and roles in West European States and societies and are looking for modern theological, cultural and social bases and concepts for their Islamic identity. Part of the European, international and interreligious project of peace and coexistence depends on the political, legal and cultural answers to their claims, as well as the answers which the Muslims themselves will encounter in their quest for inner Islamic spiritual resources for their religious identity in the modern politico-legal and cultural context of Western Europe. It is on the basis of that conviction that I ask what it means to be a European Muslim, with regard, of course, to only a few of what I deem to be the essential characteristics raised by the question.

The question of a European Muslim identity has become increasingly significant in recent years, both in academic discourse and in public debates in Europe. The topic raises a whole series of questions regarding the presence of several Muslims and Muslim communities in Western European countries since the beginning of the second half of the twentieth century up to now. It is possible to cite only a few of these questions here. We might ask, for example, if Islam can be reconciled with European values regarding civilization and culture, what the probable future holds for Muslims in Europe, what effect the presence of Muslims in West European countries will have on the future of Europe, what the implications of Muslim life in European societies are for Islam, its religious tradition and theological thought, how the Islamic identity in Europe might develop, what 'European Islam' might mean, and what challenges are facing European Muslims.

On the level of problems and theories, and against the widest possible background of world history, the present debates about Islam in Europe comprise historical, conceptual and cultural questions regarding the attitude of Islam to the fundamental achievements of the European Enlightenment of the seventeenth and eighteenth centuries, that led to secularization, belief in progress, individualization, the pluralization of values and ideologies, autonomy and the rule of reason, together with industrialization, the rise of capitalism, and the democratization of political life.[4]

Here I shall try to summarize the foregoing problems, dilemmas and topics in a single question: 'What does it mean to be a European Muslim?'

II Questions and concepts

In the present context I am primarily interested in the conceptual and religious aspect of this question. The implications of being a European Muslim are especially dependent on how we answer the questions of what Islam is, what its religious content consists of, and what its teaching is in accordance with its profound significance. If Islam may be said to consist of all traditional, customary forms of Islamic thought and action, if it contains legal solutions and prescriptions that originated in historically contingent interpretations of sharia, and further, if the normative meaning of Islam consists of all the verses of the Qur'an and traditional sayings of the Prophet, if Islam is a moral and political system of individual and social life, if Islam is religion and State at one and the same time (*din wa dawla*), if therefore Islam is perceived uncritically, both traditionally and ideologically as well as historically, then it is more or less impossible to be a Muslim in the legal, political and cultural area of Europe.

But if Islam consists of its universal messages, and if the content of Islam is that we 'believe and do good', if we follow the traditional injunctions of the Prophet in accordance with which faith (*iman*) consists of belief in God, in his angels, in his books, in his prophets, and in the Last Judgement and in divine destiny, whereby Islam comprises five religious acts (witness, prayer, fasting, mercy and pilgrimage), and whereby good deeds (*ihsan*) mean doing good and always remaining aware of the presence of God, then being a European Muslim does not imply anything so very exceptional. In other words, if we understand Islam in terms of its universal message and significance, in terms of its original religious implications, then being a Muslim in Europe is essentially the same as being a Muslim anywhere else in the world: that is, believing and doing good.

III Islam and modernity

Elsewhere reference is made to the position in terrestrial history of Muslim communities in Europe, and to the responsibility of European Muslim intellectuals with regard to the challenges faced by Muslim thought in respect of the modern world today.[5] With this in mind, it is appropriate at this point to stress that it is not sufficient to repeat, constantly and in every possible context, that in the classical period of its history Islam made its own major contribution to the theological, philosophical and scientific development of Europe. That is not the way to repair the great deficiency of critical thinking, a lack that has restricted, held back and anaesthetized Islamic thinking for centuries now. The Islamic body of thought must deal much more courageously and responsibly with the achievements of modernity. Muslim minorities that currently enjoy the fruits of democratic freedom in European societies have an historic opportunity to represent Islamic thinking more dynamically and openly in respect of creative movements oriented to modern thought. These are involvements of the kind of intensity displayed by Islam in the first centuries of its history in intellectual exchanges with other religions, philosophies and cultures. The fulfilment of an historical task of this nature is encouraged by the fact that the founding of faculties for Islamic theological studies and the training of imams and religious teachers in European universities has established the basis for a new, critical, open and plural Islamic theology oriented to dialogue, that will evolve in a European context.

IV   Dialogue and plural theology

The third major prerequisite for a Muslim body of thought in the European context is to be found in the constitutive doctrinal significance of interreligious dialogue in Islam. In consideration of the global moral, peace-oriented, environmentally-relevant and social challenges in European societies, Muslim thought can make a decisive contribution to interreligious dialogue in terms of secular standards, on the assumption that it proceeds on the basis of theological hypotheses that might be summarized as follows: no theology, which also means Islamic theology, can impose the requirement that it possesses an exclusive right to truth. Every opinion, which also means Islamic theological opinion, must be self-critical. Interreligious dialogue has to depend a relationship of equal entitlement and mutual respect among the parties to this dialogue. Every theology, which also means Islamic theology, must be prepared to learn from others. In dialogue, Islamic theology must start from a basis of responsibility for everyone in the world. Furthermore, it shares this responsibility with other religious and intellectual or spiritual traditions. Only on the basis of an open, inclusive Islamic theology is it possible to develop a vital Islamic identity that will be grounded, constructed and determined in dialogue and not in a monologue.

In Europe, the cultural identity of Muslims is largely dependent on Muslim educational systems in West European countries: that is, the cultural identity of Muslims in Europe will depend primarily on the models of education constructed by Muslims themselves in future and practised in the context of their Islamic communities. Until now, in most Muslim communities in Western Europe all Islamic education took place in accordance with models of education and concepts of interpretation of Islam which Muslim incomers had implemented by acquiring traditional educational notions, systems and institutions from the ethnic and traditional resources of distant and sentimentally relevant places of origin. If they have to use these models of education, the present generation of Muslims in West European societies cannot understand Islam in terms of universal Islamic values in a language in which they exist mentally, socially and culturally, but can perceive it only as a distant relic of ethnic folklore or as a fading sepia photographic reflection of their forebears. In general, there is an ever-growing conviction in third-generation Muslim circles that the right course to follow consists of a new form of Islamic discourse: one which opens up the possibilities of active participation in social life instead of the introversion that was characteristic of the early phases of Muslim presence in Western Europe between 1950 and 1980.

The major challenge facing Muslim communities in Western Europe in the short term in their attempts to construct their Muslim identity in this part of the world is precisely the question of their religious education in the European intellectual and historical context.[6]

V Languages

My fourth affirmation regarding the question of what it means to be a European Muslim is that Muslim communities in Western Europe need not be any kind of diaspora. In shaping their religious life and Islamic identity in Europe, they must free themselves from the ethnic, national, state, political and any other form of pastoral embrace of their so-called original Islamic communities. Muslims must mould and construct the models, systems and arrangements for their religious education in the context of their communities in Western Europe. More precisely, their religious educational institutions must be located in European countries. They must train their religious educationists, imams, teachers of religion and Islamic social workers in the Islamic educational institutions which they will run in European countries independently or within the framework of European universities. Religious education must be carried out in Islamic communities, mosques, mektebs, weekend religious courses, Islamic primary and secondary schools, madrassas and other religious and educational institutions in the languages of the third and fourth generation of West European Muslims: which means in English, French, German and other West European languages. Otherwise hundreds and hundreds of Muslim boys and girls, and young people, will be unable to understand and accept the message of Islam as part of their identity, since language (and this really should not need to be stressed) is more than a mere instrument of understanding.

VI Law and politics

The fifth major dimension of my question regarding Muslim identity in Europe concerns the possibility of leading an Islamic life within the secular and democratic, legal and political order of Europe. In this respect, two basic approaches to interpreting the Muslim perspective in Western democratic, liberal and secular societies are possible. We might follow some Muslim thinkers in seeing the modern world in Europe as excluding God completely; liberalism as a colonial ideology of capitalism; and secularism as the radical relativization of religious values and their exclusion from public life.

If we take that attitude to the modern European world, then we can give only pessimistic, negative and oppositional answers to the question of Islamic identity in Europe.

On the other hand, like a growing number of contemporary Muslim authors, theologians and thinkers, we can also take an optimistic, positive and affirmative view of Islamic identity in Europe. Then the approach is one that is presented and articulated ever more creatively, credibly and theoretically on a theological level in Muslim religious circles, and in Muslim interreligious, intercultural and political debates. This approach implies that the liberal European concept of political and cultural life ensures that Muslims as citizens enjoy all the rights and freedoms that they require to express their Muslim identity in peace and equality.

It is in this sense that Tariq Ramadan, one of the currently most quoted writers on Islam in the West, closes a study entitled *Being a European Muslim*: 'Islamic sources allow and encourage Muslims to commit themselves fully to their society while observing the prescribed legal framework ... Muslims are bound to accept a positive, responsible and constructive understanding of who they are. This is not easy, and the greatest challenge for future generations will certainly be the following: changing Muslims' own notion of themselves.'[7]

VII Conclusion

I believe, and would stress the point here, that an open attitude to Islamic identity in a secular European context, in addition to the existing arguments in theoretical and public debates, calls for much more involvement with regard to religious resources within Islam and grounds for a Muslim acceptance of the secular concept of society. The secular principle is unacceptable for Islam on a cosmological level. On a historical and political level, however, Islam originally called for a fundamental distinction to be made between the divine and the human. In this sense one might speak of an Islamic justification of secularism. The basic theological postulate in Islam is that God is neither like anyone nor like anything. That is the principle of the secularization of the world and of history. In Islam an era of history in which God constantly intervened with his revelations came to a close with Mohammed (peace be upon him and God's salvation!), and an era of history opened up during which there will be no more such interventions, and during which, if we are concerned with a revelation, we must have recourse to reason and its communicative and argumentative strategy. If no one has the right to interpose himself or herself between God and humankind as in Islam, that means that no one is entitled to speak in God's name, to represent God before humans and humans before God. We might refer here to the term '*harem*', which represents the area near religious buildings, and refers to the fact that classical Islamic culture and traditional Islamic societies always maintained an emphatic and clear distinction between sacred space and profane space. Accordingly, if there is no church in Islam, this means that Islam is a secular religion on a social level and in an institutional sense.[8]

Finally, I would like to refer to the significance of the openness of the question of what it means to be a European Muslim. Although the Islamic presence in Europe has deep historical roots, the question of the Muslim identity in Europe is, and certainly ought to be, an open question. The Islamic identity in Europe should be historically open, culturally dynamic, and religiously grounded, though in a self-critical relationship to tradition and modernity.

Translated by V. Green

Notes

1. Edward Said, *Orientalism, Western Conceptions of the Orient*, Harmondsworth, 1995, p. 6.
2. Ferid Muhić, *Islamski identitet Evrope*, Sarajevo, 2014, p. 26.
3. *Ibid.*, p. 26.
4. See Nikola Ornig, *Die Zweite Generation und der Islam in Österreich: Eine Analyse von Chancen und Grenzen des Pluralismus von Religionen und Ethnien*, Graz, 2006, pp. 67–105.
5. *Cf.* Bülent Ucar (ed.), *Imamausbildung in Deutschland: Islamische Theologie im europäischen Kontext*, Osnabrück, 2010.
6. Tariq Ramadan, *Biti evropski musliman*, Sarajevo, 2002, p. 286.
7. See also Dževad Hodžić, 'Religija i politika u sekularnom društvu', in *Islamska scena u Bosni i Hercegovini*, Sarajevo, 2011, pp. 68–76.
8. *Ibid.*.

What Does it Mean to Be A European Theologian?

ERIK BORGMAN

This article reflects on the position of European theology in the light of the fate of Sarajevo. It draws on a book written by Dževad Karahasan in 1993 during the siege of Sarajevo, and argues that European theology must respond to the discovery that at times truth and goodness can only survive by being hidden in the dark. This means that European theology cannot trust in what is generally considered revealing and enlightening, as it has done so often since the 1960s. Starting from a story by the half-Jewish, half-Serbian writer Danilo Kiš (1935–89), it is argued that theology's calling is explicitly not to be masters of, but rather beggars for, sense, meaning and the grace meaningfully to mirror God's passionate love for the ruined and scarred world that we inhabit.

I Introduction

A meeting of the editorial board of *Concilium* in Sarajevo was a meaningful event. As a city, Sarajevo is a significant landmark in the recent history of Europe. From a theological standpoint, being in Sarajevo calls for a text that does not abstractly speak about and reflect what happened and happens in Sarajevo. The city has to be witnessed to as a theological location, a *locus theologicus* in the literary sense of the word. We do not need a theology reflecting on Sarajevo, but we need a theology reflecting Sarajevo. Being in Sarajevo means being in Europe – not just at a particular place, but in a particular manner. It teaches us something about what it means to theologize in Europe.

II Intrinsic dignity

It is probably fair to say that Sarajevo changed my life. Not during the brief period of time that I spent in the city last year, but about 20 years ago. My life changed through the reading of a portrait of Sarajevo presented in 1993 by Dževad Karahasan, writer, critic and professor of literature. The book was called *Dnevik selidbe*, which means something like *Diary of Removals*. It was published in English as *Sarajevo: Exodus of a City*. The title of the Dutch translation, however, puts a slightly different emphasis on it: *Sarajevo: Portret van een in zichzelf gekeerde stad*, that is: *Sarajevo: Portrait of an Introverted City*. The Dutch edition contains pictures taken by the Dutch photographer Frank Vellenga, showing the giant curtains that during the war kept people at street level out of sight of the snipers who used to position themselves on the rooftops of apartment buildings.[1] So much for the ideal of an open city. Because of Sarajevo it started to dawn on me 20 years ago that it was not necessarily openness, but introversion, that might well be the way to keep life going.

I think that the most disturbing text in Karahasan's book is his report on the clash of expectations in a conversation with a visitor from France. This visitor was really interested in what was going in in Sarajevo under siege, as was I, as a reader of his text. He tried to find out what was happening in this first 'hot war' on the European continent after the end of the Cold War. After an intense debate, in May 1993 the Dutch government decided to send troops to Bosnia. As you will remember, this led to the handing over of Srebrenica to the Bosnian Serbs under the command of General Ratko Mladić, and the genocide of more than 8000 Muslim men and boys on 13 July 1995.[2]

In 1993 we, the Dutch, still lived in the illusion that we were part of the humanitarian vanguard of the world, but Karahasan made clear in his book how difficult it is to really understand a situation, and even to understand that you do not understand it. The Frenchman was unable to hear what Karahasan told him about life in Sarajevo, because he had already sized up the situation. He thought he already knew what it meant to be a victim of war, like Karahasan, that he knew what it meant to live with constant threats and enduring scarcity; he needed Karahasan just to fill in some blanks. As a result, Karahasan felt profoundly misunderstood. He could not provide the stories the Frenchman had clearly hoped for, and for his part could not bring across how even in extreme situations people somehow managed still to live their lives in dignity.

133

'My child has all it needs, thank God', Karahasan reports a man replying when asked why he refused baby blankets and baby clothes from UNICEF. 'What does it have?', asks Karahasan in disbelief. And the man responds: 'It has the opportunity to die in dignity.'[3] It is the most daring declaration of independence imaginable. I do not claim to understand how the man could say this, but I do know that it is profoundly true. People are not reducible to what they have or what is lacking them. They live their intrinsic dignity, for better or for worse. If necessary, in hiding.

III   Hidden secret

In a book on the history of twentieth-century Europe, Mark Mazower describes Europe with intentional irony as a 'dark continent'.[4] For a long time, Europeans routinely referred to Africa as 'the dark continent', as somewhere exemplarily violent and incomprehensibly chaotic. Mazower shows how Europe itself is the 'dark continent', paradigmatically harbouring the forces it says it wants to stay away from. And these forces are not forces of nature, to be domesticated by civilizing culture. If we read our European history honestly, we must conclude that it is the very same civilization that wants to conquer the darkness with its light that paradoxically awakens and keeps alive the violent antagonistic forces of darkness. The Enlightenment drive to discretely separate truth from falsehood, freedom from captivity, and peace from violence, makes us see the logic of war and antagonistic struggle as the very foundation of our reality. If the project is to ban the forces of darkness entirely, the supposed forces of light end up as forces of violence and destruction. We have a term for this mechanism: the dialectic of enlightenment.[5] But does it help us to escape that dialectic?

The gospel of John reports Jesus as building on solid common sense when he says: 'Anybody who does wrong hates the light and keeps away from it, for fear his deeds may be exposed. But anybody who is living by the truth will come to the light to make it plain that all he has done has been done through God' (John 3. 20–1). But the 'dark continent' Europe created situations in which what is good and true could only survive under the cover of darkness. Bringing the light to light meant losing it, getting those cultivating it scattered, arrested, and not seldom tortured and killed.

They were exposed as enemies to what truly constitutes human progress and sometimes they ended up testifying to that themselves. To quote the

Johannine Jesus again: 'This is the judgement, that light has entered the world, and men have preferred darkness to light because their deeds are evil.' (John 3. 19) In the history of the European continent, time and again the growing darkness has been mistaken for the long-awaited dawn, and as a result the light has had to hide itself in the cloak of darkness in order to simply, but paradoxically, survive.

I consider it therefore rather strange – to put it mildly – that we, European theologians, especially since the mid-1960s, seem to have tried so extremely hard to avoid even the slightest impression that we might not be on the side of what all consider to be the enlightening forces of our times. Even now, we often try to avoid any possible suspicion that there may be something to hide, that there is something deeply disturbing in the biblical message, a secret that has to remain a secret in order not to be attacked. Were we Europeans – are we Europeans not still – in a unique position to discover that God's reign should not be considered as a project or a utopian idea, but as a hidden secret?

'The Kingdom of heaven', Jesus says in the gospel of Matthew (in what seems to be the parable on secrecy): 'is like some treasure which has been buried in a field. A man finds it and buries it again, and goes off overjoyed to sell all his possessions to buy himself that field' (Matt. 13. 44). The earth is God's not because of what it clearly shows, but because of the secret it hides. In his letter to the Colossians, Paul suggests that this implies that we should be glad to be hidden as well: in his view, in their baptism Christians have died to what is usually considered life, visible at the surface, and their 'true life is a hidden one in God, through Christ' (Col. 3. 3). And Christ himself, in turn, is God's great secret 'For it is in him, and in him alone, that men will find all the treasures of wisdom and knowledge' (Col. 2. 3).

IV   The consolation of compassion

In remembrance of our dark history, we as European theologians should discover and recover and – to bring the paradox to the extreme – uncover the mystery, the secrecy of the biblical tradition. In my actual context this has a very specific urgency. In the Netherlands we are required by our various governments – the government of the country and the ministry of education, and the governments and boards of our universities – to eliminate every unclear aspect of our teaching and research. Serving the job market should be the intention and evidence-based effect of our teaching. Our research should bring clear answers to questions that are economically and politically urgent. We may very well end up with a theological curriculum that unambiguously makes sense to our world, but if that dream were to come through, who needs, who can even make sense of, the message that 'the kingdom of God is at hand' apart from those who are kept effectively out of sight in order not to disturb our view of the world?

Terry Eagleton suggests that we have been so successful in pushing the disturbing aspects of our way of life out of sight, that our societies no longer need the kind of religion Karl Marx compared to opium. We can survive on the occasional drink, the occasional party drug, and the occasional dose of therapeutic spirituality.[6]

In this situation, theology should not help to further the domestication of religion and Christianity. I am convinced that we should discover, recover and uncover the fact that biblical and post-biblical traditions are keeping a secret, and by keeping a secret are keeping us.

Dževad Karahasan entrusts his readers with a secret – a public secret, a secret he makes public, but that will always remain a secret. Karahasan tells us how in Sarajevo under siege he received a letter from a friend and how this faced him with a dilemma: 'We could not read it while there was daylight, because daytime had to be used to fetch drinking water and something to eat, and we could not read it at night, because [his] handwriting was too minute to be read by an oil lamp.'[7]

Finally, after a nightly attack that seriously injured their neighbours, making them feel even more lost and lonely, Dževad Karahasan and his wife Dragana decided to stop being responsible and did the only sensible thing: 'I lit two more oil lamps, put the letter on the table, surrounded it with all three oil lamps and started deciphering [the] handwriting. For three evenings in a row we went on to prodigiously burn oil, trying to read a letter full of friendly concern and sympathetic understanding of our problems. That extravagance left us without oil, but it renewed our hope, our feeling that we really existed … In our personal calendar, the only one that makes sense during war, we have named those three nights spent over the illegible letter of a friend the "orgy of consolation".'[8]

The simple secret is that in the midst of the darkness of our dark continent, Europeans survived by compassion and care that reminded them of their inalienable dignity through the recognition of the inalienable dignity of others. People care about us, and thus we can start to believe that we matter.

That might well liberate us from our fear for what is supposed to threaten us: other people, alien to us except in their desire to live the kind of live they consider to be good, in recognition of their dignity.

V   To speak the truth

It is this secret that Christians should be living, and that theology should think and represent in cultural debates: we live by honouring and being honoured in one another's dignity. This secret requires our full dedication, making ourselves truly vulnerable and aware of our dependency on the friendship and love that has been bestowed on us in the past, and that we may hope will be bestowed on us in the future.

To give an impression of what thinking this secret might mean, I turn to a story of the Hungarian-born writer Danilo Kiš, who was a descendant of a Jewish father and a Montenegrin Christian mother, considered himself to be a Yugoslav, and died from cancer in exile in Paris in 1989, when he was 54.[9] During his life, Kiš embodied central and often very painful paradoxes of our European history. The story in question clarifies for me what the approach of a theology that tries to be really faithful to our European experience might be.

The title of the story is 'The Game'. In the opening scene, a man peeps into the room where his son is playing, and comes to see him suddenly in a totally new way.[10] This son, whom his wife calls 'her little "Fair-Haired Boy"', suddenly looks the spitting image of the man's father, the boy's grandfather: Max Ahasuerus, an itinerant Jewish feather merchant. Inside the room the boy, Andreas, goes from painting to painting 'with his sales pitch as if wandering through the centuries', asking each and every one if they maybe want to buy some of his feathers. He thinks that they all say No, but he continues.

As his mother enters the room, the boy asks her too, with a smile and a bow: 'Can I interest you in some nice swans' feathers?' The mother silently tears the pillow, representing the merchandise, out of the boy's hands, flings it onto the bed and sends him out of the room. That evening, she tells her son a bedtime story about a king who married a Gypsy girl, who bears him a son, and then he kills her. Because, the mother says: 'if word got out that she was the boy's mother, the boy would lose the throne.

Luckily, he looked like his father, and no one could tell from the colour of his skin that he had Gypsy blood in him.'

The boy is not aware of his own role in the story, until his mother tells him how the king found his son one day 'holding a velvet and silk pillow and standing in front of a picture begging (she put up a Gypsy accent at this point): "a crust of bread, all powerful queen", he heard him say, "and a rag to cover my nakedness..." The king rushed into the room beside himself, and grabbed his son. "What are you doing, prince?", he cried. "Begging, father", said the prince. "I am tired of my toys and horses and falcons, and I am playing beggar".'

'Forget where you come from and be glad you're a prince and you will be king', the mother advises her son by telling this story. The boy finds this impossible. He understands intuitively that he will always remain a Jew, a Gypsy, an unwanted wanderer and what he really is, never at home. One might wish for such a clear insight into the mechanisms of self-mutilation in today's theology.

When the boy's mother in Kiš' story, under the impression that he is asleep, tries to leave her son's bedroom in silence, the boy asks: 'Did [the king] kill his son too?' She turns around and caressed the child tenderly: 'No', she says in a whisper without turning on the light. 'He didn't'. There is some freedom to speak the truth.

VI Being a beggar

What I am going to say next, makes me feel highly uncomfortable. At the same time, it is somehow fitting for a lay Dominican to say it in a Franciscan House of Studies (as I did, when I gave this paper in Sarajevo, where there was freedom to speak the truth).

I believe that we theologians should profess (and 'profess' should be understood here in the fully religious sense of the word) the fact that ultimately we can't remain satisfied with what have proved to be toys and horses and falcons. We should start not just to play the beggar, but to realize fully that we are beggars, dependent on the food and clothes assigned to us. In their dedication to the poor and homeless Christ, St Francis of Assisi and St Dominic of Caleruega presented an alternative to the growing trust the world was putting in the power to control, buy and sell. Francis and Dominic consciously depended on goodness and truth, powerful in that they alone could give true freedom, but powerless in that they could only be recognized freely.[11]

If we want a future for theology in Europe, we should stop trying to align ourselves with what is powerful and is commonly recognized as representing the light. We should surrender to what is weak, and abandon ourselves to what at first sight seems a dark secret. We know (surely, at least we have been told) that God has chosen what the world calls weak to shame the strong (1 Cor. 1. 27), and that 'the true light ... shines upon every man as he comes into the world ... yet the world failed to recognize him ... Yet wherever men did accept him he gave them the power to become sons of God' (John 1. 10 & 12).

In 1938, on the eve of the Shoah, the catastrophe that would re-define the very idea of what a catastrophe meant, the Jewish theologian Abraham Joshua Heschel reminded his audience in Frankfurt-am-Main that God was waiting for them to redeem the world.[12] They clearly did not do this, just as our other forebears did not, just as we have not – as yet. After he escaped to the USA, Heschel would write after the Shoah that we should learn to interpret our standing before God again as a sacrifice. We should feel 'broken-hearted, poor, needy', and thus abandon ourselves to the hidden mystery of God's presence.[13] It should make us available to become possessed by God's passion for dignity, the dignity of humans and the dignity of the universe, as the expression of his holiness. Thus we may again find (or probably better, thus we may again be found by) the secret of the redemption of the world.

Can we re-discover what it means to say that salvation does not depend on what we find in our theologies, but on whether we can allow ourselves to be found? I am by no means sure of that, but I am convinced that only then will theology have a future in Europe.

Notes

1. Dutch: D. Karahasan, *Sarajevo: Portret van een in zichzelf gekeerde stad*, Amsterdam, 1994; English: *id.*, *Sarajevo: Exodus of a City*, New York, 1994. For an image of the Dutch edition, with one of the photographs of Vellenga on the cover, see http://www.roelschuyt.nl/servo-kroatisch/.
2. For a full report of what happened, see the UN report *The Fall of Srebrenica* (1999), http://daccess-dds-ny.un.org/doc/UNDOC/GEN/N99/348/76/IMG/N9934876.pdf?OpenElement.
3. D. Karahasan, *Sarajevo: Exodus of a City*, *op. cit.*, p. 43; translation slightly modified on the basis of the Dutch edition, *Sarajevo: Portret*, *op. cit.*, p. 41.

4. M. Mazower, *Dark Continent: Europe's Twentieth Century*, Harmondsworth, 1998.

5. *Cf.* Max Horkheimer & T. W. Adorno, *Dialektik der Aufklärung: Philosophische Fragmente*, Amsterdam, 1947; ET: *Dialectic of Enlightenment*, New York & London, 1969.

6. T. Eagleton, *Culture and the Death of God*, New Haven, 2014, pp. 1–2.

7. D. Karahasan, *Sarajevo: Exodus of a City, op. cit.*, p. 44.

8. *Ibid.*, p. 42.

9. For background on Kiš, *cf.* M. Thompson, *Birth Certificate: The Story of Danilo Kiš*, Ithaca, 2013; for his view of literature and writing, see *Danilo Kiš: Gespräche und Essays*, Munich, 1994.

10. See D. Kiš, *Early Sorrows: For Children and Sensitive Readers*, New York, 1969, pp. 21–8: 'The Game'.

11. For an intriguing, if not always unproblematical, analysis of the freedom to which this leads, *cf.* G. Agamben, *The Highest Poverty: Monastic Rules and Form-of-Life*, Redwood City, 2013.

12. The text of a lecture 'delivered in March 1938 at a conference of Quaker leaders in Frankfurt-am-Main, Germany', was reprinted in A. J. Heschel, *Man's Quest for God: Studies in Prayer and Symbolism*, Santa Fe, 1954, pp. 147–51.

13. A. J. Heschel, *Man's Quest for God, op. cit.*, pp. 70–2.

Part Five: Theological Forum

The Crucified God in a Crucified Region

STIPE ODAK

The following contribution is not a conventional review but a theological reflection on the book Teologija: silazak u vražje krugove smrti: o četrdesetoj obljetnici 'Raspetog Boga' *(*Theology: Descent into Vicious Circles of Death. On the Occasion of the Fortieth Anniversary of 'The Crucified God'*), Zoran Grozdanov (ed.), Rijeka, 2014.*

Antony Gormley's sculpture entitled 'Transport' is made entirely of used nails which outline the shape of a human body. Although the body of the sculpture is made of emptiness, it is not an empty body. On the contrary, it represents the fullness of a suffering self whose borders are defined by the nails directed both inwards and outwards. The identity of Gormley's Man of Sorrow is thus a porous identity, anchored in moments of dual acceptance of pain (accepting the pain from others, and accepting the fact that one's own existence inflicts pain on others). This art-piece helped me to think more deeply about Moltmann's idea of Christian identity, which is in a permanent process of *kenosis*. His theological masterpiece *The Crucified God: The Cross of Christ as the Foundation and Criticism of Christian Theology* (1972) strongly emphasized the cross as the hermeneutical key to Christian theology, and defined real pain and suffering as a central place of theological reasoning.

The event of the cross in which the Christian God identifies Godself with those who are godless and abandoned deconstructs every tradition which seeks to project God into a domain of apathetic eternity. At the same time, that event exposes the corruption of political and social structures that create innocent victims. Moltmann's theology of the cross does not

143

start from a concept, but from a crisis. It is developed as an attempt to understand actual situations of pain and suffering and God's role in them. Although written over 40 years ago, *The Crucified God* has inspired many theological movements around the world: Liberation, Black, and Minjung theologies are some of them. Their common feature is an audacious descent into 'vicious circles of death', which is Moltmann's term for economic, political and cultural structures that do not allow humans to be humans.

The book *Theology: Descent into Vicious Circles of Death* is both an act of homage to Moltmann's classic, and an attempt to create a regional contextual theology of South-Eastern Europe. It is a collection of five essays, organized around the central idea of theology as a discipline deeply embedded in reality and developed through encounters with pain and suffering. Jürgen Moltmann himself wrote the first essay ('The Crucified God in Context'), and in it he reminds us of the actual circumstances that motivated him to write *The Crucified God*. In Moltmann's view, the theology of the cross is not simply one of many possible theologies. On the contrary, the cross is the only possible locus from which authentic Christian theology can be developed. Consequently, every cross, every place of suffering, is a cry that asks for its theological articulation.

Moltmann's programmatic ideas are further explicated in the essay 'Theology from the Concrete', by Zoran Grozdanov, who notices a conspicuous absence of contextual theologies in the area of Southern Slavic countries. That region, marked by numerous historical scars and divisions, is in many respects theologically provocative. It is a place with a long Christian, Islamic and Jewish heritage, a meeting-point of Orthodoxy and Catholicism, but also an area tainted with collective memories of violence, genocide and suffering. Moreover, it is a territory that suffered the oppression of two totalitarian regimes in the twentieth century and fell into a difficult process of transition thereafter, having been abandoned in its own post-colonial experience of an empty space between East and West. It seems almost paradoxical that the region in question never created any coherent theological tradition or school of thought that would articulate the abovementioned experiences. The reasons behind this unusual theological silence are too complex to be presented in a short notice, but it is interesting to point out two views of this problem. Zoran Grozdanov, the editor of the volume in question, suggests that adherence to the idea of a 'godly God' prevented the development of authentic contextual theologies in this region, while Ivan Šarčević, a Professor at the Franciscan Faculty of Theology in Sarajevo, claimed in his 'Pretpostavke kontekstualne teologije u BiH' (published in *Bosna Franciscana* 21 [2004], pp. 5–22, esp. 13) that the rediscovery of the 'godly God'" is actually one of the prerequisites for their development.

Although those two statements seem to be diametrically opposed, they are both correct. What Grozdanov criticizes is a theological tendency to overlook people's actual suffering on the pretext of universality or alleged religious orthodoxy. The 'godly God' that Grozdanov criticizes is an apathetic God of silence whose due worship is reflected in theological silence, that is, a complete inability to build theology on a land bathed in blood and pain. On the other hand, a problem that plagued the theology of ex-Yugoslav countries was a too frequent identification of national-ethnic and religious identity. Understood thus, God is seen as an exclusive protector of one's own group and tradition. Such a God never actually touches the real world, but remains stuck in the 'middle heaven' of human constructs (not human reality).

That is why Šarčević calls for liberation from such concepts and the rediscovery of a 'godly God' who is not constrained within national and/ or religious borders. This book aims precisely to achieve those two aims of embedding theological reflections deeply in the real suffering of the people and liberating faith from political and ideological constraints. The order in which the essays are printed shows that these goals are closely interconnected and that one cannot be achieved without the other.

The subversive aspect of Christian memory comes to light in Alen Kristić's essay. He analyzes the potential of local religious communities in Bosnia and Herzegovina to contribute to the development of humanizing and liberating political structures. His focus is on the process of 'relativization and desacralization of the political sphere', which can be carried out only by abandoning what he describes as 'utopias of national–religious ghettos', and by consciously abdicating positions of power. Kristić denounces a sinful 'metaphysical mentality' which turns religious communities into closed groups intolerant of any form of plurality. Such a mentality calls for the abandonment of the spirit of freedom in favour of unquestioning obedience, and it is detrimental to the faith and to the social engagement of believers. What he advocates is acceptance of the position of weakness and fragility, which is much more open to the plurality of life, and demonstrates a greater sensitivity to the traumas of the post-war period. One important axis of his criticism is directed towards an anxiety for religious orthodoxy, which is, in his view, a mask for enslavement to an 'apathetic God'. This particular aspect is further developed in the contribution by Entoni Šeperić, who maintains that the deafness of theological discourse to the 'orgy of death and destruction of life' is correlated with the rigidity of religious creeds. What he means can be illustrated by situations in which theologians are more dedicated to the preservation of what they understand as doctrinally correct than to the preservation of life.

Finally, Branko Sekulić criticizes the phenomenon of 'political religions', which are actually political ideologies hidden behind the mask of the sacred. Such regimes do invoke religious sentiments but, as Sekulić says, they create holes in sacred memory and fill them with egoistic interpretations. In a domain of pain and suffering, political religions demonstrate a peculiar tendency to what Sekulić describes as 'religious necrophilia', or an unordered tendency to celebrate death by detachment from life. He criticizes a tendency of religious subjects to a self-imposed feeling of victimhood, which can function only if there is a constant threat of death maintained by a selective evocation of past suffering. Consequently, everything that is different and other can be seen only as potentially destructive. Metaphorically speaking, 'religious necrophilia' is a perpetual recycling of death that never allows for the possibility of Easter and reconciliation between 'Gentiles' and 'Jews'.

These authors trace neuralgic points of identity, life and the mentality of religious communities in the former Yugoslav region, and call for God's liberation from 'vicious circles of death'. At the same time, they offer a new theological programme that tries to steer between the Scylla of apathetic religious escapism and the Charybdis of divinization of the political sphere.

The importance of a book like this can hardly be overestimated. Since an authentic contextual theology that describes the real 'nails' in the body of this crucified region is largely underdeveloped, we should applaud this pioneering attempt to fill the gap. This is both a re-reading of Moltmann's theology and a programmatic text of new regional theologies. This dual aspect can also be seen as its weak side. Some of the many topics hinted at in the text might perhaps have been developed further, and some other starting-points (not just Moltmann's) might have been chosen. Some readers might object that the book is more a prolegomenon to contextual theologies than an explication of them, but any such criticism would be insensitive to the *Sitz im Leben* of this original work. Instead of treating it as a finished project, it might be more appropriate to see it as an open letter and a call for further theological descents into 'vicious circles of death'.

Capital and Inequality: Thomas Piketty

KLAUS DA SILVA RAUPP & LUIZ CARLOS SUSIN

Thomas Piketty's *Capital in the Twenty-First Century*[1] has been described as the most important book of 2014, and perhaps of the decade (by Paul Krugman, the renowned Professor of Economics at Princeton University, who was awarded the Nobel Prize in Economics in 2008).

Piketty's explanations of the dynamics of the accumulation and distribution of capital (that is, the concentration of wealth and inequality) have disturbed many economists, for we live in a world where the neo-classical economics associated with neo-liberalism in politics is still the predominant economic school of thought. His book is considerably indebted to the French 'Annales' School of History, to Fernand Braudel's perspective of '*la longue durée*' (or 'long duration', reflecting thousand-year-long changes), and to World-System Analysis, in the sense that he analyzes complex social issues in a long-term period and in a global context, especially with regard to capitalism and inequality.

From an inter-disciplinary angle, theology has a lot to say about the content of this book, from the biblical perspective of the good news for the poor to modern Catholic social teaching and its concerns about economic justice. This is especially true when Pope Francis is exhorting everyone to be aware of and reject the capitalist economy and its social consequences, and meets the leaders of social movements inside and outside the Vatican. In terms of a 'see-judge-act' methodology, it is crucial to understand the economic and social context of the real world first before theologians can illuminate those facts in the light of their own sources, and contribute to practical actions to deal with that context.

After explaining some important economic concepts and laws, Piketty analyzes a long-term historical series of data that his research group has collected about income, wealth and poverty in several countries. This research covers three centuries of data in more than 20 countries, including the United States, Japan, Germany, France, the United Kingdom, Italy and Canada, which are classed as the seven largest developed countries in terms of their nominal gross domestic product. Therefore this book is based on historical facts rather than on common sense or on theoretical models. As an evidence-based work, it lends credibility to Piketty's ideas.

Piketty's central thesis is that 'when the rate of return on capital exceeds the growth of output and income, capitalism automatically generates arbitrary and unsustainable inequalities that radically undermine the meritocratic values on which democratic societies are based' (p. 1). To prove this statement, he first defines the rate of return on capital ('r') and the rate of growth of the economy ('g'). The first rate ('r') includes profits, dividends, interest, rents, and other income from capital; and the second ('g') is the annual increase in income or output. Piketty then shows that over the past three centuries 'r' reached an average of five per cent, whereas 'g' was much lower than this percentage over the whole period of three hundred years. This means that the wealth of the wealthiest individuals has grown at a higher rate compared to the whole economy. The richest really got richer, and the poorest really got poorer, so to speak.

These facts allow Piketty to conclude that there is an immanent law of the system: if 'r' is greater than 'g', the richest will be permanently richer, and in the long run inequality will be based not only on differences of income, but on inherited fortunes. In economies where the rate of return on capital is higher than the rate of growth of the economy, inherited wealth (the outcome of capital accumulation) will always grow faster than acquired wealth (the outcome of labour income).

Piketty's conclusions challenge the fallacy according to which financial success is guaranteed to those who strive in life. In fact, the children of the richest usually have the best opportunities, and their wealth grows more rapidly. On the other hand, sons and daughters of the poorest work hard for their wages, and are usually able to save much less than the richest. This is not accidental, but the law of the system working properly. In other words, inheritance (fortunes accumulated in the past) predominates over savings (wealth accumulated in the present).

Piketty understands that capitalism is not truly democratic, but definitely creates considerable inequality. But he also implies that socialism is not the best alternative to overcome inequality, as the history of Eastern Europe might be said to have demonstrated. This relates Piketty to Marx, yet he cannot be interpreted as a new Marx. He offers a very profound analysis of the current economic and social context of the real world, but he does not propose an economy of transition. It is also central to his thesis that 'there are nevertheless ways democracy can regain control over capitalism and ensure that the general interest takes precedence over private interests, while preserving openness and avoiding protectionist and nationalist reactions' (p. 1). Piketty suggests a progressive taxation of income, and especially of capital income (mainly of big fortunes), as the best alternative to regulating capital and diminishing inequality. He also believes that that form of taxation is a crucial component of the social State. Those who earn more, own more, or consume more should pay higher taxes than others, and this system should replace proportional taxation (the same rate) for everyone.

Of course, taxation is a political and philosophical question. The study of history shows us how important it has been to the main revolutions since the Ancien Régime, or even before Christianity. All the synoptic gospels present the pericope in which Jesus is asked whether it was just or not to pay taxes to Caesar. This is an old question, and it is still relevant today, especially if we consider Jesus's answer that we should give to Caesar what belongs to Caesar, and to God what belongs to God. According to Christian faith, everything belongs to God, who created everything in his love and justice. Therefore, taxes should be defined and paid under principles that guarantee justice for all, so that God's will can be accomplished at the actual level of our social, political and economic relationships.

The main idea of Piketty's book is very much associated with the principle of the common good, that is, with social justice. This is a principle of modern Catholic social teaching present in all its documents since *Rerum novarum*. In *Pacem in terris*, Pope John XXIII stated that the common good could never exist fully unless human beings were taken into account at all times, and said that every single person had the right to share in it. He also said that at times justice and equity could demand that those in power should pay more attention to the weaker members of society, because of disadvantages (inequalities) in social structures.

Another essential principle related to the main idea of Piketty's book is the preferential option for the poor, which first inspired liberation theology in its origins in Latin America. The richest getting richer and the poorest getting poorer is a sad but true reality that the capitalist mode of production imposes on modern societies. Even though there is formal (not necessarily substantial) democracy in most capitalist societies, and though there have been some improvements in the life of the poor, the abyss between the richest and the poorest is still unbridgeable, and this is offensive to basic humanism and to the foregoing principles. It is a serious social sin that calls for repentance and liberation.

Brazil's economy, though not included in Piketty's research and book, is a good illustration of this disparity between the richest and the poorest. According to the United Nations, 17 million people (out of 20 million) surpassed the line of extreme poverty and hunger in the country in the past 12 years. Yet Brazil's Central Bank tells us that the earnings of banks and other agents of the financial market have reached unprecedented levels in the country's history. The amount invested in public social programmes was very much below the profits of financial institutions, and taxation of the latter is completely regressive, mainly compared with taxation of goods and services consumed by families.

Piketty's work provides a strong empirical basis for what Pope Francis states in his recent Apostolic Exhortation *Evangelii gaudium*. He says that 'while the earnings of a minority are growing exponentially, so too is the gap separating the majority from the prosperity enjoyed by those happy few' (n. 56). Therefore he tells the Catholic world to stand up against 'the economy of exclusion' (nn. 53–4), 'the new idolatry of money (nn 55–6), 'a financial system which rules rather than serves' (nn. 57–8), and 'the inequality which spawns violence' (nn. 59–60). In fact, capital is very much a false goddess that requires many sacrifices of human lives on its altar, especially the poorest and those affected by the destructive temptations of consumerism, which is a scandal to Christian faith. Pope Francis wishes to persuade people to take practical action in the face of inequality, and calls on everyone to ensure 'generous solidarity' and 'the return of economics and finance to an ethical approach which favours human beings' (n. 58).

Finally, this is an interesting area for further study, focusing on the applicability of Piketty's thesis and its relation to Catholic theological ethics, as attempted briefly in this review. For instance, there is much room for interdisciplinary research into taxation as an instrument of economic justice in the light of modern Catholic social teaching. One research topic could be the possibility of defining 'just taxation', like the magisterium's definition of a 'living wage'.

Notes

1. *Capital in the Twenty-First Century* by Thomas Piketty, translated from the French by Arthur Goldhammer, Cambridge, MA. & London, 2014 has four parts and 16 chapters: Part One (Income and Capital): (1) Income and Output, (2) Growth, Illusions and Reality; Part Two (Dynamics of Capital/Income Ratio): (3) The Metamorphoses of Capital, (4) From Old Europe to the New World, (5) The Capital/Income Ratio over the Long Run, and (6) The Capital-Labour Split in the Twenty-First Century; Part Three (The Structure of Inequality): (7) Inequality and Concentration: Preliminary Bearings, (8) Two Worlds, (9) Inequality of Labour Income, (10) Inequality of Capital Ownership, (11) Merit and Inheritance in the Long Run, (12) Global Inequality of Wealth in the Twenty-First Century; Part Four (Regulating Capital in the Twenty-First Century): (13) A Social State for the Twenty-First Century, (14) Rethinking the Progressive Income Tax, (15) A Global Tax on Capital, and (16) The Question of the Public Debt.

Gender and the Croatian Bishops' Conference

JADRANKA REBEKA ANIĆ & JADRANKA BRNČIĆ

In recent years rapid globalization and cultural change have confronted the Catholic Church with inescapable challenges and a demand for openness and discussion, which has seemed especially acute in the areas of sex and gender. The Church has responded with the documents of Vatican II, and various papal and other initiatives, including the Extraordinary Synod called by Pope Francis. Under the guise of concern for young people, the reaction of the bishops of Croatia to certain local political measures has disclosed an apparent lack of the requisite degree of understanding of, and of the necessary extent of debate on relevant questions with regard to gender.

I Introduction

The new millennium is characterized by global networking, and by more rapid and intense cultural changes than in the past. With regard to doctrine and pastoral concerns, the Catholic Church is faced with new challenges when trying to assess these changes, especially in the area of human sexuality. The 'memory of the future'[1] proposed by the Second Vatican II Council, as well as the commemoration of the fiftieth anniversary of the publication of the encyclical *Ecclesiam suam* (1964) by Pope Paul VI, in reaction to these points at issue, invite us to use dialogue as our method, and to promote a culture of discussion.

One of these challenges for the modern Church consists of anthropological questions which, in ecclesiastical circles, are simplified and reduced to the question of 'gender ideology'. Are we actually, as was stated in the '*Relatio Synodi*' of the third extraordinary assembly of the

Synod of Bishops, in the middle of an 'anthropological transformation'[2] or, as the Catholic writer Gabriele Kuby claimed, in the middle of an 'anthropological revolution'? Should we, as a memorandum of the same Synod, its *'instrumentum laboris'*,[3] suggests, deal with these changes by avoiding widespread condemnation in order to respond polemically to the challenges; or should we, like Gabriele Kuby, consider all those concerned with these questions to be 'sworn enemies' of the Catholic Church?[4]

Pope Francis encourages open dialogue and discussion within the Church through the extraordinary Synod of bishops. In some churches, including the Catholic Church in Croatia, there is no dialogue. We are trapped by a polarized and politicized debate on health education in schools where it is only right that the idea of 'gender' should play an important role.

The *'Relatio Synodi'* does not mention 'gender ideology', but it is the main subject of the message of the Croatian Bishops' Conference to young people. Discussions about the concept of 'gender' began in Croatia when the anti-discrimination law was passed in 2008. In ecclesiastical circles, it is not thought necessary to interpret the term as it is understood in scientific and political discourse on 'gender'. Instead, it is read as a form of code for homosexuality, with no reference to the fact that the question of homosexual rights is covered by the concept of sexual orientation. The mistrust between the Catholic Church and the Social-Democratic party, which, by circumventing judicial procedures, wanted to introduce health education into schools in the 2012/13 school year, provoked the appearance in Croatian public opinion of the theory that a 'cultural war' was in question here. This was the context in which the Croatian bishops published their document addressed to young Catholics.

II The Croatian bishops' message

In ecclesiastical circles, the syntagm 'gender ideology', which is close to Marxist ideologies, in the context of an ideological division on the one hand, and attempts to homogenize society, on the other hand, seems more appropriate than the term 'gender theories'. After all, the non-negotiability of the syntagm 'gender ideology' is guaranteed by certain church documents and by the authority of the Pontifical Council for the Family and of the Congregation for the Doctrine of Faith. Gabriele Kuby's books were translated, conferences were organized where she spoke, and theologians have even repeated and studied her hypotheses, all with the consent of the Croatian bishops. Moreover, even serious theological works published abroad were unable to make an impact on the discussion about gender and 'gender ideology'. Critical theological voices were rapidly reduced to silence and even punished. Calling in question the concept of 'gender ideology' has been considered to be treason towards the Church and national interests. The bishops of the Croatian Episcopal Conference published an open letter concerning 'gender ideology' on 15 October 2014, during the third extraordinary general assembly of the Synod of Bishops. The document was designed as a Message to Young People and was entitled: 'Man and Woman He Made Them!'.[5] Archbishop Hranić introduced the document at a press conference on 23 October, remarking that it mainly concerned a doctrinal message and not guiding principles for pastoral practice, that the Message was about 'gender ideology', and that the Church, when it evangelizes and teaches, warns us against values opposed to the Gospel. We must see the Message, it seems, as the bishops' effort to 'protect' young Christians against the mind-set and spirit of 'gender ideology'. Consequently, the intention of the Message is to reveal strategies of evil concealed in 'gender ideology' and to protect young believers.

This Message to young people suggests that they should reject the word 'gender', because a 'dangerous' even diabolical 'ideology' of the 'culture of death' is hidden behind it. The Message supposes that it is a question of a perfidiously conceived, gradually implemented, and radically inhuman 'anthropological revolution' which, according to the Croatian bishops, has settled on marriage conceived as a union between man and woman and on the family similarly intimately linked by love, in order to replace them with arbitrary types of 'loving relations', deny the natural innateness of masculine and feminine, and finally, lead to the 'death of humankind' as such.

Even though there are certainly problematic developments win the field of gender theories, this can never be an excuse for a crude and blundering approach to questions of gender, or for referring to 'world conspiracy' while using methods that can only be called intimidation.

III   Gender theories or 'gender ideology'?

Therefore the Croatian bishops' Message does not deal with gender theories, but with 'gender ideology' defined as identical with 'gender theory, gender perspective, gender-ideology and so on'. Classifying all the terms in which the word 'gender' appears as 'gender ideology' makes it possible to evade defining the term 'gender' and avoids having to analyze the different ways in which the term is used in a variety of scholarly and scientific disciplines and international documents. The intention is to discredit them all equally. This is why the bishops warn us that the defenders of 'gender ideology' conceal their real intentions behind talk of noble efforts and a fight against discrimination, and on a commitment to establishing freedom, equality and tolerance.

The bishops' Message suggests, then, that you can't mention gender without representing 'gender ideology'. This suggestion is problematical for a certain number of reasons and is tantamount to identifying sex with gender. The aim of this identification is, amongst others, it seems, to deny the problem of the role of genders, to whose development the Church has certainly contributed throughout history. In fact, the ruling principle of the Message is that maintaining the traditional distinction between masculine and feminine models of behaviour, and not only in the sphere of sex, has to be understood as a divine commandment, because when God created man and woman he is said to have created their social role (the bishops call this 'natural law') at the same time.

The bishops also pigeon-hole 'gender perspective' or 'gender viewpoint' in the context of 'gender ideology', although in international documents this viewpoint means the methods to establish and guarantee equality of opportunity for women and men in all the areas of life. The German 'Justice and Peace' Commission considered gender perspective compatible with Catholic teaching, and more suitable than the so-called feminist perspective that puts the emphasis on women.[6] We have to ask why the Croatian bishops locate this perspective, that takes into account the well-being of women and men, under the denominator 'gender ideology' and consider it detrimental to women and men and hostile to the family. And why does their Message omit to mention that the Holy See, in the Declaration of the Fourth International Conference on women, which accepts the notion of gender (if it is based on the biological sexual identity, female or male), already distances itself from a 'determinist biological understanding that all roles and relationships between the two sexes are fixed in one static model'?[7] Surely their Message clearly represents that very same determinist understanding?

IV   'Protecting' young people

The bishops of the Croatian Bishops' Conference state that 'the only correct definition of human nature is found in Holy Scripture', whereas any such definition simply does not exist in the Bible. The bishops want 'to protect' young believers at any price from the idea of gender, which 'reduces the human person', while offering them no more than their own arbitrary interpretation of gender as the only correct one.

This raises certain questions. Why do the bishops want to protect only young believers and not all young people? Are they protecting the young with this kind of message, or are they just making them afraid? How can this message be understood by young people, who, at the same time as being Catholics, identify themselves as intersexual, bi-sexual, trans-sexual or gay? Are the bishops really protecting them, and, if so, from whom or what? Are they protecting young people from the violence of those who can't accept their differences?

We can also ask what the bishops expect of young people? What should they be? Is a message of this type the best way to protect them? Surely it is preferable to educate young people to judge in an independent way in a world that is changing rapidly and permanently? Should their consciences be formed by the dictates of the Church, or formed so that they can take responsibility for their opinions and their lives as a whole? Does this message encourage young people to read, explore, think, and enter into dialogue, or to flee and return to the Catholic enclave with high walls behind which they will be protected from the bad world and from the 'perfidies of the devil' (*perfidiae diaboli*), as the Dean of the University of Zagreb Catholic Theology Faculty, theologian and bio-ethician Tonči Matulić describes discourse about gender in his commentary on the Message? Does all this mean that Catholic theology has run its course and no longer has the strength to engage with currents of contemporary thought and the diverse theories behind it?

V   A defensive document

In addition to its arbitrary use of the term 'gender ideology', the text of the Message shows a certain number of other weaknesses, including generalization, misrepresentation of basic facts, simplified reference to the book of Genesis, and quotations taken out of context. The main problem is that the Message, on the one hand, does not communicate all the information on gender theories, and, on the other hand, offers a peculiarly dualist view of reality.

Because positive evaluations and uses of the terms 'gender' and 'gender theories' exist in Catholic theology, a more differentiated approach is necessary.[8] Defensive documents in the face of the evolution of modern society and of the possible development of the Church and of theology, do not offer reference points for relevant discussion, but reject everything in a pessimistic and sceptical way without any real confrontation and readiness to engage in dialogue. The addressees are unknown, lost as they are in an impersonal mass of gender ideologues in which everyone can be included.

VI Conclusion

Regina Ammicht Quinn quite rightly believes that it is dangerous to think with the aid of critical gender categories. Not because this gives rise to ideologies, but because ideologies can be laid bare.[9] To call self-evident security or naturally given truths in question is a hazardous enterprise. In other words, gender is a dangerous concept because it requires knowledge, constant monitoring, and a highly-nuanced approach. Since this is a difficult route to follow the tendency is to choose something much easier: generalized condemnation and rejection. But that is totally useless. You can't stop research in every possible field. You cannot debate a subject proficiently if you only recognize scientific and scholarly (including theological) research that supports your own opinions, and entirely ignore ideas that could call them in question. The fear, disorientation and frustration that prevail in the face of the challenges posed by the equality of women and men and questions to do with bi-sexuals, homosexuals, transgender people, and so on, will not be resolved by diabolizing the people who explore and ask these questions. And isolation doesn't help. You can only advance in dialogue by confrontation, and by listening to the other side until you understand what they are saying.

Translated by Felicity Leng

Notes

1. J.-H. Tück (ed.), *Erinnerung an die Zukunft: Das Zweite Vatikanische Konzil*, Freiburg im Breisgau, 2013.
2. Paragraph 5, http://www.vatican.va/roman_curia/synod/documents/rc_synod_doc_2014 1018_relatio-synodi-familia_it.html.

3. Paragraph 127, http://www.vatican.va/roman_curia/synod/documents/rc_synod_doc_ 20140626 _instrumentum-laboris-familia_fr.html.

4. Gabriele Kuby, *Gender: Eine neue Ideologie zerstört die Familie*, Kislegg, 2014.

5. http://www.mladi.hbk.hr/article.php?id=1475.

6. http://www.justitia-et-pax.de/jp/publikationen/pdf/guf_104.pdf

7. The Final Statement of the Holy See at the Women's Conference in Beijing, http://www.its.caltech.edu/~nmcenter/women-cp/beijing3.html.

8. See, e.g., the 'gender' issue of *Concilium*: Gender in Theology, Spirituality and Practice (2012:4); Marianne Heimbach-Steins, *'...nicht mehr Mann und Frau': Sozialethische Studien zu Geschlechterverhältnis und Geschlechtergerechtigkeit*, Regensburg, 2009; Jadranka Rebeka Anić, *Kako razumjeti rod? Povijest rasprave i različita razumijevanja u Crkvi*, Zagreb, 2011.

9.*Cf.* Regina Ammicht Quinn, 'Dangerous Thinking, Gender and Theology', *Concilium* (2012:4), London, 2012, pp. 23–4.

Contributors

DINO ABAZOVIĆ is a sociologist of religion, and Extraordinary Professor in the Faculty of Political Science of Sarajevo University, a member of the Sociology Committee in the Social Sciences Department of the Academy of Sciences and Arts of Bosnia and Herzegovina. His books include: *Bosanskohercegovački muslimani između sekularizacije i desekularizacije* (*Muslims from Bosnia and Herzegovina between Secularization and Desecularization,* Sarajevo, 2014), *Religija u tranziciji* (*Religion in Flux,* Sarajevo, 2010), and *Za naciju i Boga: sociološko određenje religijskog nacionalizma* (*For the Nation and God*, Sarajevo, 2006), and he has edited several symposia.

Address: Fakultet političkih nauka
Skenderija 72
71000 Sarajevo
Bosnia & Herzegovina
Email: abazovicd@fpn.unsa.ba

JADRANKA REBEKA ANIĆ, SSFCR is responsible for research at the Ivo Pilar Institute of Social Sciences – Regional Centre of Split in Croatia. She has taught in the universities of Zagreb, Split and Sarajevo. She is President of the Croatian section of the European Association of Women for theological research and has published, among other books: *Više od zadanoga: Žene u Crkvi u Hrvatskoj u 20. stoljeću* (2003), *Žene u Crkvi i društvu* (2010) and *Kako razumjeti rod? Povijest rasprave i različita razumijevanja u Crkvi* (2011).

Address: Institut društvenih znanosti Ivo Pilar – Područni centar Split
Poljana kraljice Jelene 1/I
HR-21000 Split
Croatia
Email: rebeka.anic@pilar.hr

MILE BABIĆ was born on 26 November 1947 in the village of Družnovici, Bosnia and Herzegovina. He is a Bosnian Franciscan and a Professor of theology and philosophy. He graduated in history of literature; obtained PhDs in theology (the Christology of Theodoret of Cyrus) and in philosophy (Hegel's Philosophy of Law). He has been lecturing at the Franciscan Theologate in Sarajevo since 1997. He is the editor-in-chief of *Miscellany Jukic* and a Professor of religious studies at the University in Sarajevo. His research subjects include the Theodoret of Cyrus, John Duns Scotus, Nicolaus of Cusa, G. W. F. Hegel, and contemporary literature, theology and philosophy. Since 2013, he has been a member of the Editorial Board of *Concilium*.

Address: Franjevačka teologija Sarajevo
Aleja Bosne Srebrene 111
BiH-71000 Sarajevo
Bosnia & Herzegovina
Email:dekan.babic@gmail.com

ERIK BORGMAN (Dr E.P.N.M.) was born in Amsterdam in 1957. He holds the Cobbenhagen Chair at Tilburg University, The Netherlands, teaching and researching in the fields of systematic Theology and Public Theology. He is married with two daughters and a Lay Dominican. Borgman studied philosophy and theology at the University of Nijmegen. His doctoral dissertation was on the different forms of liberation theology and their relation to Western academic theology (higher teaching thesis 1990). From 1998 until 2004 he worked for the Dutch Province of the Order of Preachers to study and keep alive the theological heritage of Edward Schillebeeckx. He published *Edward Schillebeeckx: a Theologian in his History. Volume I: A Catholic Theology of Culture* (London & New York, 2003). From 2000 until 2007 he worked at the interdisciplinary Heyendaal Institute for theology, sciences and culture at Radboud University, Nijmegen; from 2004 onwards as its academic director. Borgman is a member of the Editorial Board of *Concilium*.

Address: Department of Culture Studies
PO Box 90153
NL - 5000 LE Tilburg

The Netherlands
Email: E.P.N.M.Borgman@uvt.nl

JADRANKA BRNČIĆ was awarded a doctorate for her thesis on the interpretation of biblical texts according to Paul Ricœur at the Faculty of Philosophy of Zagreb, where she works. She also teaches at the Protestant Theology School at Zagreb. She has published, amongst other books: *Anđeli* (1998, 2003), *Biti katolik još* (2007), *Franjina Pjesma stvorenja* (2012), S*vijet teksta: Uvod u Ricœurovu hermeneutiku* (2012) and *Zrno gorušičino: Hermeneutičko čitanje o dabranih biblijskih perikopa* (2014).

Address: Filozofski fakultet
Ivana Lučića 3
HR-10000 Zagreb
Croatia
Email: jbrncic@ffzg.hr

ZORAN GROZDANOV is a PhD candidate in the Department of Philosophy of the Faculty of Humanities and Social Sciences, University of Zagreb, Croatia. He graduated in philosophy, history and theology in Zagreb and Osijek (Croatia). In 2010–11, he studied at the University of Tübingen (Germany), where he wrote his dissertation under the supervision of Jürgen Moltmann. He has edited and written contributions for *God before the Cross: Festschrift in Honour of Jürgen Moltmann* (Rijeka, 2007); *Dangerous Memories and Reconciliation: Contextual Reconsideration of Religion in Post-Conflict Society* (Rijeka, 2010), *Theology: Descending into Vicious Circles of Death* (Rijeka, 2014.). He teaches at the University Centre for Protestant Theology, University of Zagreb.

Address: Teološki fakultet Matija Vlačić Ilirik
Radićeva 34
HR-10000 Zagreb
Croatia
Email: carnaro@gmail.com

ALEKSANDAR HEMON (born 9 September 1964) is a Bosnian American fiction writer, essayist, and critic. He is the winner of a MacArthur Foundation grant. He has written five books: *The Book of My Lives* (New York, 2013); *Love and Obstacles: Stories* (New York, 2009); *The Lazarus Project: A Novel* (New York, 2008), which was a finalist for the National Book Award and the National Book Critics Circle Awards, and was named as a *New York Times* Notable Book and *New York* magazine's No. 1 Book of the Year; *Nowhere Man* (New York, 2002), also a finalist for the National Book Critics Circle Award; and *The Question of Bruno: Stories* (New York, 2000). He frequently publishes in *The New Yorker*, and has also written for *Esquire*, *The Paris Review*, the Op-Ed page of the *New York Times*, and the Sarajevo magazine *BH Dani*.

DŽEVAD HODŽIĆ ist Professor in the Faculty of Islamic Studies in Sarajevo. He has taken part in a number of international conferences (in Bosnia and Herzegovina, Hungary, Austria, Germany, Macedonia and Australia and the USA). He has published several books, including *Uvod u islamsku etiku* (*An Introduction to Islamic Ethics*, Sarajevo, 1999), *Kud a ide Islamska zajednica – poste restante* (*Where is the Islamic Community Headed – Poste Restante?*, Sarajevo, 2005), *Odgovornost u znanstvenotehnološkom dobu, TUGRA* (*Responsibility in the Age of Sciences and Technologies*, Sarajevo, 2008), and *Religija i znanost u bioetičkom ključu* (*Religion, Science and Bioethics*, Zenica, 2012), and numerous scientific works, He is a member of the Board of the Bioethics Union of Bosnia and Herzegovina.

Address: Fakultet islamskih nauka
Ćemerlina 54
71000 Sarajevo
Bosnia & Herzegovina
Email: finhodzic@gmail.com

PANTELIS KALAITZIDIS studied theology in Thessaloniki, and philosophy in Paris. His doctoral thesis was on Greekness and Anti-westernism in the Greek theology of the 1960s. He has published three books, and over 70 articles, mainly in the areas of the eschatological dimension of Christianity, the dialogue between Orthodoxy and modernity, theology and modern literature, religion and multiculturalism, religious nationalism and fundamentalism, issues of renewal and reformation in Eastern Orthodoxy, and post-modern hermeneutics of Patristics. He has been a Visiting Scholar at Holy Cross Greek Orthodox School of Theology, Boston, Princeton Theological Seminary, and Princeton University, and Senior Research Fellow at the Center for World Catholicism and Intercultural Theology, DePaul University, Chicago, IL. For the last 14 years he has been the Director of the Volos Academy for Theological Studies, a church-related institution dealing with contemporary issues for Eastern Orthodoxy. He teaches Systematic Theology at the Hellenic Open University, and at St Sergius Institute of Orthodox Theology in Paris (as Visiting Professor). His most recent book, *Orthodoxy and Political Theology*, was published by WCC Publications (Geneva, 2012).

Addresss: Volos Academy for Theological Studies
P.O. Box 1308
GR-38001 Volos
Greece
Email: pkalaitz@acadimia.org

DžEVAD KARAHASAN (Duvno, 1953), is a Bosnian-Herzegovinian man of letters, essayist, novelist, drama specialist and Professor at the Sarajevo Academy of Scenic Arts. He has been Visiting Professor at several European universities (Salzburg, Innsbruck, Berlin and Göttingen). He spent 2007/2008 at the Wissenschaftskolleg in Berlin. He has been awarded a number of European prizes, including the Herder Prize (1999), an honorary award of the Heinrich-Heine-Gesellschaft (2012) and the Goethe Medal of the Goethe Institute (2012). He has published several works, including *Der östliche Diwan*, (1989), *Tagebuch der Aussiedlung* (1993), *Schahrijars Ring* (1996) and *Der nächtliche Rat* (2005). Many of his books have been translated into European and other world languages.

Address: Augusta Brauna 1
BiH – 71000 Sarajevo
Bosnia & Herzegovina
Email: dzevad.karahasan@gmx.at

Contributors

SAROJINI NADAR (PhD) is a full professor and leader of the Gender and Religion Programme at the University of KwaZulu-Natal, South Africa. As a transdisciplinary researcher, she has researched and published widely in the field of feminist biblical hermeneutics, with a special focus on HIV and AIDS, gender-based violence, masculinity and sexuality. She has also researched and published on theories of feminism in Africa, and has more recently been engaged in research into social justice and higher education systems.

Address: Director: Gender and Religion Programme
School of Religion, Philosophy and Classics
Memorial Tower Building
Howard College Campus
University of KwaZulu-Natal
South Africa
Email: nadars@ukzn.ac.za

STIPE ODAK is a doctoral candidate in theology and religious studies at the Catholic University of Leuven. He graduated with a degree in theology from the Catholic Faculty of Theology in Zagreb (Croatia), and in Sociology and Comparative Literature at the same university. He later earned the licentiate in theology (STL) from KU Leuven with highest honours. His doctoral project, supported by the Belgian National Fund for Scientific Research (FNRS), explores the relationship between religion and the collective memory of conflicts.

Address: Rue des Blancs Chevaux 3/206
1348 Louvain-la-Neuve
Belgium
Email : stipe.odak@gmail.com

DANIEL FRANKLIN PILARIO CM is Professor and Dean of the St Vincent School of Theology, Adamson University, Manila, the Philippines. He has published *Back to the Rough Grounds of Praxis* (Leuven, 2005), co-edited several anthologies, among them *Mediations in Theology* (Leuven, 2003); *PCP II Twenty Years After* (Quezon City, 2014), and contributed

165

articles to philosophical and theological journals. His research areas include theological anthropology, inculturation, interreligious dialogue, theological method and socio-political theory. He is a founding member and former President of DAKATEO (Catholic Theological Society of the Philippines). He is a member of the Editorial Board of *Concilium*.

Address: St Vincent School of Theology
Adamson University
221 Tandang Sora Avenue
P.O. Box 1179
1151 Quezon City
Philippines
Email: danielfranklinpilario@yahoo.com

REGINA AMMICHT QUINN, Dr theol. habil, is Professor of Ethics at the International Centre for Ethics in the Sciences (IZEW) of Tübingen University and its spokesperson. In 2013 she founded the Gender and Diversity Research Department at Tübingen University and is currently one of its two Directors. Her fields of research are fundamental principles and applications of ethics, especially political ethics, ethics and questions of gender, ethics and security in modern companies, and clashes of values and hierarchies of values within and between 'religious' and 'secular' companies.

Address: Internationales Zentrum für Ethik in den Wissenschaften (IZEW)
Universität Tübingen
Wilhelmstr. 19
D – 72074 Tübingen
Germany
Email: regina.ammicht-quinn@uni-tuebingen.de

KLAUS DA SILVA RAUPP is a Brazilian attorney-at-Law also working as a theologian. He holds a Master's Degree in Theology from the Pontifical Catholic University of Rio Grande do Sul (Brazil). He has been teaching in the field since 2007, specializing in systematic theology and Catholic social teaching; He is now on leave to continue his graduate studies at the PhD level in the USA.

Address: 74 Oakland St
Boston, MA
02135
USA
Email: klaus.raupp@bc.edu

SUSAN A. ROSS is Professor of Theology and Chair of the Department of Theology at Loyola University, Chicago. Her research is in the areas of feminist theology and ethics, and especially sacramental theology, theological anthropology, and sexuality. Her most recent book is *Anthropology: Seeking Light and Beauty* (Liturgical Press, 2012). She is a past President of the Catholic Theological Society of America and a Vice-President of *Concilium*.

Address: Department of Theology
Loyola University Chicago
1032 West Sheridan Road
Chicago, IL
60660
USA
Email: sross@luc.edu

PERO SUDAR was born in Bare (Bosnia and Herzegovina) in 1951, and was ordained priest in 1977 in the archdiocese of Vrhbosna (Sarajevo). In 1985, he was awarded a higher teaching degree in canon law, which he has taught since 1986 in the Catholic Theological Faculty in Sarajevo. Until 1989, he was Head of Studies of the seminary of the archdiocese. In 1993, he was consecrated a suffragan bishop of Vrhbosna. Bishop Sudar promotes the movement 'Catholic Schools for Europe'. He has published several articles in scholarly journals, including 'Crkva između prava čovjeka i prava vjernika' (*Teološke teme*, Sarajevo, 1991, pp. 209–32); 'Gegen den Strom schwimmen. Kirchliche Versöhnungsarbeit in Bosnien-Herzegowina' (in *Wende-Zeit: Wie Christen Europa verändern*, Freising,

1999, pp. 77–85); 'Con vivere per vivere' (*AVE*, Rome, 2002); 'Bosnia ed Erzegovina: un modello possibile?' (*Monte Senario* 7 (2003), pp. 48–56).

LUIZ CARLOS SUSIN is a Capuchin friar, a Doctor of Philosophy of the Gregorian University, and currently Secretary General of the World Forum of Liberation Theology and a member of the Editorial Board of *Concilium*. He is Professor of Systematic Theology of the Higher Institute of Theology and Franciscan Spirituality and at the Pontifical Catholic University of the Rio Grande do Sul.

Address: Rua Juarez Távora, 171.
Porto Alegre-RS
ZC: 91520-100
Brazil
Email: lcsusin@pucrs.br

UGO VLAISAVLJEVIĆ is Professor of Philosophy and Ontology in the Faculty of Humanities and Arts, University of Sarajevo. He is a member of the editorial board of the journal *Transeuropéennes* (Paris), and former President of PEN Centre Bosnia and Herzegovina (2006–9). He has published many books, including *Phenomenological Constitution of European Union* (1995), *Lepoglava and University* (2003), *War as the Greatest Cultural Event: Towards a Semiotics of Ethnonationalism* (2007).

Address: Department of Philosophy,
University of Sarajevo
Obala Kulina Bana 7/II
71 000 Sarajevo
Bosnia & Herzegovina
Email: vlaisugo5@gmail.com

MIROSLAV VOLF is the Henry B. Wright Professor of Theology at Yale University Divinity School as well as Founder and Director of the Yale Center for Faith and Culture. He was educated in his native Croatia, United States, and Germany. He earned doctoral and post-doctoral degrees (with highest honours) from the University of Tübingen, Germany. He has written or edited 15 books and over 70 scholarly articles. His most significant books include *Exclusion and Embrace* (1996; winner of Grawemeyer Award in Religion, and one of *Christianity Today*'s 100 most important religious books of the twentieth century); *Allah: A Christian Response* (2011), *Do We Worship the Same God?* (2012); and *A Public Faith: On How Followers of Christ Should Serve the Common Good* (2011).

Address: Yale Center for Faith and Culture
409 Prospect St
New Haven, CT
06511-2167
USA
Email: miroslav.volf@yale.edu

MARIE-THERESE WACKER is Professor for Old Testament and Gender Research in Theology at the Faculty of Catholic Theology, University of Münster, Germany. Her research areas include biblical monotheism, Hellenistic Judaism and gender relations in monotheistic religions. She is, together with Luise Schottroff, co-editor and author of *Feminist Biblical Interpretation: A Compendium of Critical Commentary on the Books of the Bible and Related Literature* (Grand Rapids, 2012).

Address: Seminar für Exegese des AT
Johannisstrasse 8-10
D-48143 Münster
Germany
Email: wacker.mth@uni-muenster.de

FELIX WILFRED was born in Tamilnadu, India in 1948. He was for many years professor at the State University of Madras, and President of the Faculty of Arts in the same university. He was a member of the International Theological Commission of the Vatican when Cardinal Joseph Ratzinger was the chairperson. As visiting professor he has taught at the Universities of Frankfurt, Münster, Nijmegen, Boston College,

Ateneo de Manila and Fudan University, Shanghai. He had the singular honour of having been appointed by the Government of India as the first holder of its newly-established Chair of Indian Studies at Trinity College, Dublin. His researches and field studies today cut across many disciplines in humanities and social sciences.

Address: Asian Centre for Cross-Cultural Studies
40/6A Panayur Kuppam Road, Panayur
Sholinganallur Post Chennai–600119
India
Email: felixwilfred@gmail.com

CONCILIUM
International Journal of Theology

FOUNDERS
Anton van den Boogaard; Paul Brand; Yves Congar, OP; Hans Küng;
Johann Baptist Metz; Karl Rahner, SJ; Edward Schillebeeckx

BOARD OF DIRECTORS
President: Felix Wilfred
Vice Presidents: Thierry-Marie Courau; Diego Irarrázaval; Susan Ross

BOARD OF EDITORS
Regina Ammicht Quinn (Frankfurt, Germany)
Mile Babić (Sarajevo, Bosnia-Herzogovina)
Maria Clara Bingemer (Rio de Janeiro, Brazil)
Erik Borgman (Nijmegen, The Netherlands)
Lisa Sowle Cahill (Boston, USA)
Frère Thierry-Marie Courau (Paris, France)
Hille Haker (Chicago, USA)
Diego Irarrázaval (Santiago, Chile)
Solange Lefebvre (Montreal, Canada)
Sarojini Nadar (Durban, South Africa)
Daniel Franklin Pilario (Quezon City, Philippines)
Susan Ross (Chicago, USA)
Silvia Scatena (Reggio Emilia, Italy)
Jon Sobrino SJ (San Salvador, El Salvador)
Luiz Carlos Susin (Porto Alegre, Brazil)
Andreś Torres Queiruga (Santiago de Compostela, Spain)
João J. Vila-Chã (Portugal)
Marie-Theres Wacker (Münster, Germany)
Felix Wilfred (Madras, India)

PUBLISHERS
SCM Press (London, UK)
Matthias-Grünewald Verlag (Ostfildern, Germany)
Editrice Queriniana (Brescia, Italy)
Editorial Verbo Divino (Estella, Spain)
EditoraVozes (Petropolis, Brazil)
Ex Libris and Synopsis (Rijeka, Croatia)

Concilium Secretariat:
Asian Centre for Cross-Cultural Studies,
40/6A, Panayur Kuppam Road, Sholinganallur Post, Panayur, Madras 600119, India.
Phone: +91- 44 24530682 Fax: +91- 44 24530443
E-mail: Concilium.madras@gmail.com
Managing Secretary: Arokia Mary Anthonidas

Concilium Subscription Information

February	**2015/1:** *Religion and Identity in Post-Conflict Societies*
April	**2015/2:** *Young Catholics Reshaping the Church*
July	**2015/3:** *Globalization and the Church of the Poor*
October	**2015/4:** *Theology, Anthropology and Neuroscience*
December	**2015/5:** *Silence*

New subscribers: to receive *Concilium 2015* (five issues) anywhere in the world, please copy this form, complete it in block capitals and send it with your payment to the address below.

Please enter my subscription for *Concilium 2015*

Individuals
____ £50 UK
____ £72 overseas and Eire
____ $95 North America/Rest of World
____ €85 Europe

Institutions
____ £72 UK
____ £92 overseas and Eire
____ $110 North America/Rest of World
____ €135 Europe

Postage included – airmail for overseas subscribers

Payment Details:
Payment must accompany all orders and can be made by cheque or credit card
I enclose a cheque for £/$/€____ Payable to Hymns Ancient and Modern Ltd
Please charge my Visa/MasterCard (Delete as appropriate) for £/$/€ ____

Credit card number _____

Expiry date _____

Signature of cardholder_____

Name on card _____

Telephone _____ E-mail _____

Send your order to *Concilium*, Hymns Ancient and Modern Ltd
13a Hellesdon Park Road, Norwich NR6 5DR, UK
E-mail: concilium@hymnsam.co.uk
or order online at www.conciliumjournal.co.uk

Customer service information
All orders must be prepaid. Subscriptions are entered on an annual basis (i.e. January to December). No refunds on subscriptions will be made after the first issue of the Journal has been despatched. If you have any queries or require information about other payment methods, please contact our Customer Services department.

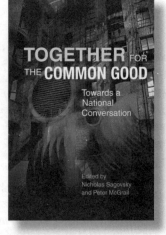

Mission on the Road to Emmaus:

Constants, Context and Prophetic Dialogue
Edited by Cathy Ross and Stephen B. Bevans

Aimed at scholars and students of missiology in the UK, US and world-wide, here is a wide-ranging study of mission and theology in today's world. A stellar cast of contributors in this book consider missions through the lens of 'prophetic dialogue'.

The authors try to bring a fresh approach to the subject of mission – introducing some newer themes (identity, creation, migration) and offering a different perspective on some older themes by grouping them in this way.

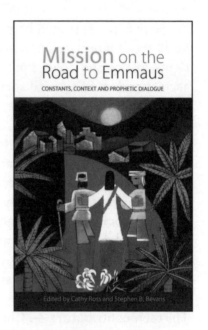

978 0 334 04909 8   Paperback   £25.00

Cathy Ross is the Director of OxCEPT at Ripon College Cuddesdon.
Steve Bevans is Louis J. Luzbetak, S.V.D., Professor of Mission and Culture
at Catholic Theological Union, Chicago, USA.

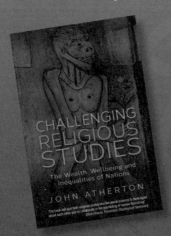